THE BOOKS OF

Zechariah AND *Haggai*

THE LORD REMEMBERS

By

Kurt Kennedy, M(BS), D.Min.

All scripture references are from the King James Bible

Requests for copies or information should be addressed to:

kennedykt@yahoo.com

ISBN: 978-0692570074

True Word Press

I would like to thank Dr. Paul Genung for the many hours he spent in proofreading this work.

This book is dedicated to Ava Grace, my little bird.

CONTENTS

THE BOOK OF ZECHARIAH

The Lord Remembers

Preface

The book of Zechariah is one of the most visionary books in all the Bible. The name Zechariah means "The LORD remembers". Zechariah is contemporary with the prophet Haggai (Ezra 5:1-2; 6:14). He was a Levite born in Babylon and like Jeremiah and Ezekiel before him he was both prophet and priest.

When Cyrus the great gave the decree for the Jews to return back to the land Zechariah was among those who returned to Israel with Zerubbabel and Joshua the high priest (Ezra 1:2-4; cf. Isa. 44:28 cf. Neh. 12:1, 16). Zechariah is a young man at the beginning of his ministry (Zech. 2:4), which started two months after Haggai delivered his first sermon. Haggai the prophet and Zechariah's messages were delivered at the same time to the same group of people, the time following Babylonian captivity to a remnant of Jews seeking to rebuild their lives. While Haggai's message is one of rebuke, Zechariah gives them encouragement, motivating them to rebuild the temple. Because of their respective ministries the people completed building the temple in four years.

11

The main focus of the book is that of the coming Messiah as a means to comfort the children of Israel and as Zechariah's name suggests[1], the LORD remembered his covenant relationship to the Jews and He would restore and bless them.

This book is filled with visions, Messianic prophesies, angelic beings, signs and the voice of GOD. In eight visions recorded in the first six chapters he predicts the overthrow of the Gentile world powers, the judgment of the apostate Jews because of their rejection of Christ, the cleansing, restoration and glory of a remnant and the future prosperity of Jerusalem.

Zechariah records some of the most amazing prophecies concerning our blessed LORD. His entry into Jerusalem on an ass (Zechariah 9:9), His betrayal by Judas for thirty pieces of silver (Zechariah 11:12-13) and His death as the stricken Shepherd (Zechariah 13:7).

Zechariah and Haggai along with Malachi will be the last prophets of God to speak. Following their ministries there will be 400 silent years until the opening of the New Testament when John the Baptist comes heralding the coming Kingdom.

---

[1] The LORD remembers

Like many of the righteous prophets before him, according to our LORD in Matthew 23:35 Zechariah was murdered between the Temple and the Altar.

The Outline of the book is as follows:

<u>Chapters 1-6 Zechariah receives 8 visions.</u>

First vision is that of a man riding upon a red horse among the myrtle trees (1:1-17). The meaning, God is not pleased with the Gentile nations that are at rest while His people suffer and the temple lies in shambles. The Gentile nations will be punished and His people restored.

Second vision is of the four horns and the four Carpenters (1:18-21). The meaning is judgment on the nations that afflict Israel.

Third vison is of a man with a measuring line (Chapter 2). The meaning, God's future blessing on restored Israel.

Fourth vision is of the cleansing and crowning of Joshua the high priest (Chapter 3). The meaning, the Priesthood representative of the nation cleansed and restored.

The fifth vision of a candlestick of gold and two olive trees (Chapter 4). By the spirit of God Zerubbabel will see the completion of the temple.

The sixth vision is of a flying roll (Chapter 5:1-4). The meaning is divine judgment on those who break the Laws of God and the role Babylon will play as the mother of harlots.

Seventh vision is of a woman in an ephah (Chapter 5:5-11). The meaning is the removal of Israel's national sin for rebellion against God; it goes back to Shinar or Babylon where it originated.

The eighth vision is of four chariots (Chapter 6:1-8). The meaning, divine judgment on Gentile nations, and the restored priesthood.

Chapters 7 & 8 are four messages given by Zechariah. They are given in response to a delegation that came to Jerusalem to ask the nation whether they should continue to fast in remembrance of Jerusalem's destruction. The question implied to discontinue the self-imposed religious observance of fasting. The first message given by Zechariah is one of rebuke. (7:4-7). The second message is of repentance (7:8-14). The third message is of restoration (8:1-17). The fourth message is one of rejoicing (8:18-23).

Chapters 9-14 consist of two burdens that look forward to the Messianic King and Kingdom. Chapters 9-11 refer to the first advent of the Messiah but also outlines Israel's prophetic history to the end times. Chapters 12-14 look forward to the glorious appearing with emphasis on His enthronement and Millennial Reign the destruction of Israel's enemies and Israel as head of the nations.

The Historical Setting

God had said to His people that they would be in captivity in Babylon for 70 years (Jer. 25:11, 12). Once the seventy years of captivity came to a close God would see to the overthrow of the Babylonian city by the Persians, under the leadership of King Cyrus. It was King Cyrus that made the decree for the Jews to return to their homeland (2 Chron. 36:22, 23 cf. Ezra 1:1, 2). A remnant of God's people returned into the land of Jerusalem seeking to rebuild the temple the house of worship. Within two years of God's people coming into the land, the foundation of the temple was laid (Ezra 3:8-13). However, upon the completion of the foundation to the house of the LORD there rose up in the land adversaries who resisted the work of the LORD from the time of King Cyrus all the way to the second year of King Darius, a time totaling over 14 years (Ezra 4:5, 24). It was at this time that the LORD calls Haggai and Zechariah to begin their ministries (Haggai 1:1; Zech. 1:1). Their calling from the LORD is to motivate the people in the land to continue the building of the temple. Haggai will do this through rebuke and Zechariah will do so through motivating them concerning the promises of God and His return to them one day. Because of both Haggai's and Zechariah's ministries they will complete the temple in just four short years.

One important factor in interpreting this book is the fact that even though historically the temple is built, there is no record of the glory of the LORD descending or entering the temple[2]. The comparison between the glory of the temple of Solomon and the temple at the time of Zechariah is not pleasant (Haggai 2:3 cf. Ezra 3:10-13). The LORD therefore in both Haggai and Zechariah continually points to a future temple in which the glory of the LORD will reside once again (Haggai 2:5-9 cf. Zech. 6:12-15 cf. Ezek. 43:1-9). It is the hope of this future temple that is mentioned in Haggai and becomes the main theme throughout the book of Zechariah[3].

---

[2] As it had done under Solomon's Temple (1 Kings 8:10-11).
[3] Also the events before and after the building of this future temple are dealt with in detail as well.

THE TEMPLES OF GOD

Glory of the Lord descends at the building (1 KINGS 8:10-11)

Glory of the Lord departs prior to the destruction (EZEKIEL 9-11)

Solomon's Temple

Destroyed by fire
2 KINGS 25

HAGGAI 2:3
EZRA 3:10-13

Temple under Ezra
(Haggai & Zechariah)

ZECHARIAH 9:9

Herod's Temple

Destroyed by fire (70 A.D.)
MATTHEW 24:2

2 THESSALONIANS 2:3,4
DANIEL 9:27
MATTHEW 24:15

Tribulation Temple

Destroyed by fire

EZEKIEL 43-48
HAGGAI 2:5-9
ZECHARIAH 6:12-15

Millennial Temple

Glory of the Lord descends and enters the eastern gate (EZEKIEL 43:1-6)

CHAPTER ONE
A Man among the Myrtle Trees

In the eighth month, in the second year of Darius, came the word of the LORD unto Zechariah, the son of Berechiah, the son of Iddo the prophet, saying, (Zechariah 1:1)

Second Year of Darius (1): As was mentioned in the previous section adversaries in the land had halted the building of the temple for approximately 16 long years (Ezr. 4:5, 24). It was not until the second year of the king Darius that God raises up Zedekiah and Haggai (Hag. 1:1). Haggai begins his ministry 2 months after he gives his first address.

The LORD hath been sore displeased with your fathers. Therefore say thou unto them, Thus saith the LORD of hosts; Turn ye unto me, saith the LORD of hosts, and I will turn unto you, saith the

LORD of hosts. Be ye not as your fathers, unto whom the former prophets have cried, saying, Thus saith the LORD of hosts; Turn ye now from your evil ways, and from your evil doings: but they did not hear, nor hearken unto me, saith the LORD. Your fathers, where are they? and the prophets, do they live for ever? But my words and my statutes, which I commanded my servants the prophets, did they not take hold of your fathers? and they returned and said, Like as the LORD of hosts thought to do unto us, according to our ways, and according to our doings, so hath he dealt with us. (Zechariah 1:2-6)

A Warning to the People of God about Their Past (2-6): The cry from God to His people at the outset of Zechariah's ministry is for Israel to remember their fathers and how they did not harken unto the voice of the prophets and kept not the commandments of the LORD and God has dealt with them accordingly. The admonition is for the people to get to work again; for the LORD will not hold them guiltless for their lack of fortitude in building the house of the LORD.

Upon the four and twentieth day of the eleventh month, which is the month Sebat, in the second year of Darius, came the word of the LORD unto Zechariah, the son of Berechiah, the son of Iddo the prophet, saying, I saw by night, and behold a man riding upon a red horse, and he stood among the myrtle trees that were in the bottom; and behind him were there red horses, speckled, and white. Then said I, O my lord, what are these? And the angel that talked with me said unto me, I will shew thee what these be. And the man that stood among the myrtle trees answered and said, These are they whom the LORD hath sent to walk to and fro through the earth. And they answered the angel of the LORD that stood among the myrtle trees, and said, We have walked to and fro through the earth, and, behold, all the earth sitteth still, and is at rest. (Zechariah 1:7-11)

The Man Among the Myrtle Trees (7-11): By a night vison Zechariah sees a man riding upon a red horse. The man upon the red horse is seen standing among myrtle trees and behind him were red horses, speckled horses and white horses (8). The man on the red horse is an angel of whom Zechariah asks, "What are these?" (9). Then the angel of the LORD tells Zechariah, "These *are they* whom the LORD hath sent to walk to and fro through the earth (10). These angelic horses take note (the angel speaking) that all the earth sitteth still and is at rest (11). This is to indicate that all the Gentile nations that have persecuted Israel are at rest in the earth in contrast to God's people who, while in their homeland are still suffering having a city without walls and no house of worship. The idea of these horses going "to and fro through the earth" is that of showing dominion. When Abram was brought into the Promised Land he was told to *"Arise, walk through the land in the length of it and in the breadth of it; for I will give it unto thee."* (Genesis 13:17) This was a symbolic act that showed his dominion over the land that God was giving to him. When Satan stood with the sons of God before the LORD, the LORD asked Satan, *"From whence comest thou? And Satan answered the LORD, and said, From going to and fro in the earth, and from walking up and down in it."* (Job 2:2) Again this is to show the dominion that Satan had as usurper of the earth. He was flaunting this authority in the face of God. Boasting in the face of the LORD that all the world is following him as the god of this world (2 Cor. 4:4). However, much to the surprise of Satan the LORD points out that there was one that was not following his evil ways, for the LORD says unto Satan, "… Hast thou considered my servant Job, that there is none like him in the earth, a perfect and an upright man, one that feareth God, and escheweth evil?" (Job 2:3). So then while these chapters have a historical setting surrounding the rebuilding and establishing of Jerusalem as the place of the house of God, they have a far more reaching significance when the LORD of all the earth reclaims that which is rightfully His, the reclaiming of the earth.

Then the angel of the LORD answered and said, O LORD of hosts, how long wilt thou not have mercy on Jerusalem and on the cities of Judah, against which thou hast had indignation these threescore and ten years? And the LORD answered the angel that talked with me with good words and comfortable words. So the angel that communed with me said unto me, Cry thou, saying, Thus saith the LORD of hosts; I am jealous for Jerusalem and for Zion with a great jealousy. And I am very sore displeased with the heathen that are at ease: for I was but a little displeased, and they helped forward the affliction. Therefore thus saith the LORD; I am returned to Jerusalem with mercies: my house shall be built in it, saith the LORD of hosts, and a line shall be stretched forth upon Jerusalem. Cry yet, saying, Thus saith the LORD of hosts; My cities through prosperity shall yet be spread abroad; and the LORD shall yet comfort Zion, and shall yet choose Jerusalem. (Zechariah 1:12-17)

How Long will the LORD Withhold His Mercy (12-17): The angel of the LORD cries out to GOD saying, "how long wilt thou **NOT** have mercy on Jerusalem and the cities of Judah... these three score and ten years?" (12). The angel of the LORD is referring to the seventy years they have been in Babylonian captivity suffering the judgment of the LORD. It was anything but "rest" that the angel of the LORD desired for these Gentile nations who have been afflicting God's people.

The LORD answers with "good words and comfortable words" which are seen in the remainder of these verses. He starts off with saying, "I am very sore displeased with the heathen that are at ease..." (15). Notice also that the LORD says He was just a "**LITTLE** displeased" but these heathen nations "helped forward that affliction" (15); the heathen did above and beyond what the LORD had called them to do.

The LORD'S direct response to the inquiry of the angel of the LORD in verse twelve is in verses sixteen and seventeen, "Therefore thus saith the LORD I am returned to Jerusalem with mercies: my house shall be built in it , saith the LORD of hosts, and a line shall be stretched upon it. ...the LORD shall yet comfort Zion and shall yet choose Jerusalem". These verses are given as encouragement to continue the building of the temple of God and it is words like these that motivated the people to complete the temple in just four short years.

Then lifted I up mine eyes, and saw, and behold four horns. And I said unto the angel that talked with me, What be these? And he answered me,

These are the horns which have scattered Judah, Israel, and Jerusalem. And the LORD shewed me four carpenters. Then said I, What come these to do? And he spake, saying, These are the horns which have scattered Judah, so that no man did lift up his head: but these are come to fray them, to cast out the horns of the Gentiles, which lifted up their horn over the land of Judah to scatter it. (Zechariah 1:18-21)

Four Horns and Four Carpenters (18-21): These two visions happen at the same time as the previous vision of the horses. The four horns are clearly defined as those Gentile nations that "scattered Judah, Israel and Jerusalem." The Carpenters are those who have come to "fray" the horns, "to cast out the horns of the Gentiles..." (21).

Concerning the interpretation of the four horns and the four carpenters I have not resolved in my mind their identity. If pressed I believe it is representative of those nations that **HAVE** scattered God's people. I believe Zechariah's vision is looking back at what had historically taken place; not at something that is yet to take place. The historical setting as mentioned at the outset of this study is that of the return of the remnant of Israel following the Babylonian captivity under the decree of King Cyrus. The horns then are those who **HAVE** scattered the nations. Israel represented as the Northern Tribes were the first to be scattered. They were scattered by Assyria's army as recorded in 2 Kings 17:1-19:37. The Southern Tribes were the last to be scattered, and they by the Babylonian armies as recorded in 2 Kings 24, 25. These would seem to make up two of the four horns. The remaining two would be those who were major players in the scattering of Israel, Judah and Jerusalem; Egypt and Syria. Syria was instrumental in assisting the scattering of the Northern Tribes and Egypt in Southern Tribes. God's people have been continually warned about making alliances with Egypt, because they are not to be trusted (2 Kings 18:21-24).

As to the identity of the four carpenters, I believe it is the historical setting that gives us the interpretation of these four. First, they are carpenters; carpenters build, which is exactly what the decree of King Cyrus declared: *"Thus saith Cyrus king of Persia, The LORD God of heaven hath given me all the kingdoms of the earth; and he hath charged me **to build him an house at Jerusalem**, which is in Judah".* *(Ezra 1:2)*. This rebuilding of the temple is historically recorded in the book of Ezra. Ezra records the events surrounding the rebuilding of the temple following the Babylonian captivity, from the laying of the foundation to the completion of the Temple. It is during this time that four key people are used in building the house of worship. In the first wave of remnants who returned to the land to build were Joshua the high priest and Zerubbabel, both of which are mentioned throughout Ezra. The next two individuals that are key in the rebuilding of the Temple are Haggai and Zechariah. Mentioned extensively throughout Ezra is Zerubbabel and Joshua (Jeshua) as is the prophets Haggai and Zechariah; these men are all instrumental in the rebuilding of the temple. Notice the wording of verse 21, "but these are come to fray them..." this would seem to me to indicate the ministry of Zerubbabel, Joshua, Haggai and Zechariah.

Thus, it would seem, given the historical context, the four horns are Syria, Assyria, Egypt and Babylon and the four carpenters are those involved in the building of the Temple, Joshua the high priest, Zerubbabel, Haggai and Zechariah.

For added thought on the subject the following are some other interpretations on these puzzling verses.

The Four Horns and Four Carpenters:

Interpretation One:

The four horns merely representing the four quarters of the earth: Israel being surrounded by her enemies, i.e. her enemies are threatening her on every side. This however gives us no interpretation as to who are the carpenters.

Interpretation Two:

The four horns are the four Gentile world powers that Daniel mentions: Babylon, Medio-Persia, Greece and Rome (Daniel 2), with each of these nations becoming the carpenter as they conquered the previous world power until the final CARPENTER Jesus Christ comes to deliver Israel from all Gentile dominion.

Interpretation Three:

The vision of Zechariah is dealing with current affairs at the time of Zechariah. The four horns are the four surrounding people that opposed the building of the temple: The Samaritans in the north, Ammonites to the east, Edomite's to the north and the Philistines to the west. The four carpenters would be the four prominent people in the building of the temple: Zerubbabel, Joshua, Haggai and Zechariah.

Interpretation Four:

The vision of Zechariah is dealing with current affairs as in the previous interpretation. The only difference would be that the horns were more national than individual people groups. So the four horns would be those that "HAVE" scattered Judah, Israel and Jerusalem, with no futuristic view. These nations were Syria, Assyria, Egypt and Babylon; with the interpretation of the carpenters being the same (Zerubbabel, Joshua, Haggai and Zechariah).

Interpretation Five:

This interpretation is similar to interpretation two in that the horns are the four world empires that have "scattered" God's people given by Daniel: Babylon, Medio-Persia, Greece and Rome. However, as to the four carpenters, they would be four horses that are involved in the reclaiming of the earth by our LORD. They are the spirits of heaven that stand before the LORD, represented also by the four chariots (see Zech. 6:1-8). These would help play a role in toppling all the Gentile powers and the LORD establishing His Kingdom (Daniel 2:44, 45) and would seem to correlate to the four horsemen in Revelation 6. The four horsemen of Revelation corresponding to the first four seals of the book that is opened containing all the judgments that bring about the overthrow of the Gentile powers (Revelation 6).

A Man among the Myrtle Trees
OVERVIEW

- The angelic horses (horsemen) are part of the LORD'S heavenly army (2 Kings 6:16). They are those who will take part when the LORD begins to have His Day on the earth as is recorded, among other places in the Book of Revelation (chapter 5-11)

- These angelic hoses (horsemen) desire to avenge the cause of Israel on the earth, having seen all the heathen nations being at "rest" while God's people suffer (vs. 11 cf. 15). Their desire of them to avenge Israel is seen by their response to the LORD saying, "how long wilt thou NOT show mercy on Jerusalem and on the cities of Judah" (12).

- The LORD gives "good and comforting words" concerning the desire of the horsemen to avenge the nations that suppress God's people in verses 16-17. Notice He does not give a timeline as to when He will accomplish this. The "good and comforting words" are as follows:

    o I am returned to Jerusalem with mercies (16)
    o My house shall be built in it (16)

o A line shall be stretched forth upon Jerusalem (16)
o My cities through prosperity shall yet be spread abroad (17)
o The LORD shall yet comfort Zion (17)
o The LORD shall yet choose Jerusalem (17)

CHAPTER TWO
A Survey of the Land

I lifted up mine eyes again, and looked, and behold a man with a measuring line in his hand. Then said I, Whither goest thou? And he said unto me, To measure Jerusalem, to see what is the breadth thereof, and what is the length thereof. And, behold, the angel that talked with me went forth, and another angel went out to meet him, And said unto him, Run, speak to this young man, saying, Jerusalem shall be inhabited as towns without walls for the multitude of men and cattle therein: For I, saith the LORD, will be unto her a wall of fire round about, and will be the glory in the midst of her. (Zechariah 2:1-5)

The Desire to Build (1-5): Once again these visions seem to be transpiring one after another. In this vision Zechariah sees a man with a measuring line in his hand (1). Notice that it is a measuring line[4], something used in relation to building. Before any building can take place the first order of business is to survey the land. This is what is happening in this chapter. The rebuilding of the Temple at the present time of Zechariah's ministry is what is in view; however we will see this vision has a far reaching fulfillment to the future building of the coming Millennial Temple. Zechariah finds out the man is going to measure Jerusalem and find its circumference (2). Stretching a line over Jerusalem was formerly used to mean destruction (2 Kings 21:13), it is now being stretched over Jerusalem to rebuild (Job 38:5). The angel that had been talking and interpreting the visons to Zechariah goes out and meets another angel who he tells to run and give a message to the man with the measuring line in his hand. The message given is that of a future glory in which Jerusalem shall be inhabited as a town without walls, a town in which the LORD shall be a wall of fire round about and a place where His glory shall sit in the midst of her (4-5). It would seem that once the Millennium is established and the temple built therein, that there will be a pillar of cloud by day and a pillar of fire by night for protection (see Isa. 4:5-6, Ex. 13:21-24). The Temple

---

[4] Notice also the angel that measured the Millennial Temple in Ezekiel (40:3, 41, 42).

that is in view is the Millennial Temple, when the glory of the LORD will return and sit in the Temple once again (See Ezek. 43:1-6).[5]

Ho, ho, come forth, and flee from the land of the north, saith the LORD: for I have spread you abroad as the four winds of the heaven, saith the LORD. Deliver thyself, O Zion, that dwellest with the daughter of Babylon. For thus saith the LORD of hosts; After the glory hath he sent me unto the nations which spoiled you: for he that toucheth you toucheth the apple of his eye. For, behold, I will shake mine hand upon them, and they shall be a spoil to their servants: and ye shall know that the LORD of hosts hath sent me. (Zechariah 2:6-9)

The Apple of God's Eye (6-9): Once again historically we see God is calling His people back from the land of the north, from the land of Babylon. The enemies of Israel always come from the north or the south due to the fact that the Arabian Desert is to the east and the Mediterranean Sea is to the west. Thus, God is calling His people back from the land of their captivity, Babylon. When Cyrus made the decree to return back into the land, not all of God's people returned immediately. However another

---

[5] This is not a prophecy of our LORD coming into the temple for His glory was vailed in a robe of flesh.

wave did return as recorded in Ezra 8. Similar commands are given in Jeremiah 50:8, 51:6. However, once again in the yet future, Israel will need to flee from the land of the north, Babylon (Revelation 18:1-5). Once again showing that while these verses do have a relevance historically they also have a yet future fulfillment.

The LORD will avenge those nations that have spoiled God's people the apple of His eye (8). For the LORD will shake His hand of judgment on those nations that spoil God's people making those nations a spoil to those that were their servants (9). This is recording events leading up to the establishment of the LORD's house, things that have to transpire in order for the building of the yet future temple of the LORD. The apple of the eye is an expression to mean that God cherishes them above all others (Deut. 32:10).

Sing and rejoice, O daughter of Zion: for, lo, I come, and I will dwell in the midst of thee, saith the LORD. And many nations shall be joined to the LORD in that day, and shall be my people: and I will dwell in the midst of thee, and thou shalt know that the LORD of hosts hath sent me unto thee. And the LORD shall inherit Judah his portion in the holy land, and shall choose

Jerusalem again. Be silent, O all flesh, before the LORD: for he is raised up out of his holy habitation. (Zechariah 2:10-13)

The LORD is Risen Out of His Holy Habitation (10-13): The singing and rejoice is due to the King of kings and the LORD of lords coming to deliver and dwell with His people (See Isaiah 12). A foretaste of this was when our LORD entered Jerusalem while He was on earth (Matthew 21:5-9). Throughout these verses the prophetic announcements about the LORD coming into the land is meant to be an encouragement to the people to rebuild the temple. The LORD will return and dwell in the midst of them (10-11 cf. Ezek. 43:7-9; Zech. 8:3). The LORD dwelling in the midst of His people is one aspect of the Abrahamic Covenant, they are GREAT because of who is dwelling in their midst (Gen. 12:1, 2). The LORD will inherit Judah his portion in the land (12 cf. Ezek. 45:1-7). The LORD arising out of His Holy habitation is an issue of the LORD beginning to have His day, the Day of the LORD (see Isa. 2:21; 3:13). The LORD'S coming from His holy habitation is the issue of Him coming from heaven in which He arises to come to earth; to begin to have "His Day" (13 cf. Deut. 26:15; Jer. 25:30).

The Apple of God's Eye
OVERVIEW

- This chapter is the amplification of Zechariah 1:16 *"Therefore thus saith the LORD; I am returned to Jerusalem with mercies: my house shall be built in it, saith the LORD of hosts, and a line shall be stretched forth upon Jerusalem."* The LORD's desire to have a house build for Him is the issue and the focus. The reason for this focus is because historically this is the need at the time of Zechariah's ministry. However, our LORD is looking far beyond the historical building of the temple to a yet future temple that He will build and fulfill His desire to dwell in the midst of His people.

- Before the building process can take place a survey of the land needs be done. Thus, Zechariah sees a man with a measuring line in his hand, to measure Jerusalem (1-2).

- The building of this yet future temple will see the glory of the LORD once again reside with His people:

  o "For I saith the LORD ... will be the glory in the midst of her" (5)

- o "For lo I come and I will dwell in the midst of thee, saith the LORD." (10)
- o "… I will dwell in the midst of thee …" (11)
- o "And the LORD shall inherit Judah his portion in the holy land and shall choose Jerusalem again." (12)
- o See Ezekiel 43:1-6
- o God's desire to dwell in the midst of His people:
  - Original Creation (Isaiah 40:22)
  - His people Israel (Ex. 25:1-9 cf. Rev. 21:3)
  - Believer today (I Cor. 6:19)

- Zechariah closes this chapter with a vision of the LORD arising from His holy habitation. A look into the yet future time when the LORD will arise to accomplish the desire to dwell in the midst of His people in Jerusalem (13).

CHAPTER THREE
Joshua the High Priest and the Cleansing of the Nation

And he shewed me Joshua the high priest standing before the angel of the LORD, and Satan standing at his right hand to resist him. And the LORD said unto Satan, The LORD rebuke thee, O Satan; even the LORD that hath chosen Jerusalem rebuke thee: is not this a brand plucked out of the fire? Now Joshua was clothed with filthy garments, and stood before the angel. And he answered and spake unto those that stood before him, saying, Take away the filthy garments from him. And unto him he said, Behold, I have caused thine iniquity to pass from thee, and I will clothe thee with change of raiment. And I said, Let them set a fair mitre upon his head. So they set a fair mitre upon his head, and clothed him with garments. And the angel of the LORD stood by. And the angel of the LORD protested unto Joshua, saying, Thus saith the LORD of hosts; If thou wilt walk in my ways, and if thou wilt keep my charge, then thou shalt also judge my house, and shalt also keep my courts, and I will give thee places to walk among these that stand by. Hear now, O Joshua the high priest, thou, and thy fellows that sit before thee: for they are men wondered at: for, behold, I will bring forth my servant the BRANCH. For behold the stone that I have laid before Joshua; upon one stone shall be seven eyes: behold, I will engrave the graving thereof, saith the LORD of hosts, and I will remove the iniquity of that land in one day. In that day, saith the LORD of hosts, shall ye call every man his neighbour under the vine and under the fig tree. (Zechariah 3:1-10)

The Cleansing of Joshua the High Priest (1-10): The historical setting is once again of important significance. Joshua the high priest with Zerubbabel are the key people during the ministries of Zechariah and Haggai. The cleansing of the land and the people are what is in view, being represented by Joshua the high priest (vs. 2 cf. vs. 9-10). The land and the people had become filthy by their apostate behavior, from idolatry to failing to keep the law of God. They have also become filthy due to their Babylonian captivity. It is this filthiness that Satan had been directly involved in, making them unfit for the plan and purposes of God. However, as this chapter will show, the LORD will rebuke Satan and cleanse His people and the land as is represented by the removing of Joshua's filthy garments and placing on him clean garments (4-5). This cleansing will take place when the LORD will send forth His BRANCH (8). With the seven spirits of God at His disposal the LORD will remove the iniquity of the land and cleanse the people, establishing His kingdom over the earth (9-10).

Satan standing to resist Joshua (1-2): Satan is the adversary of God and His people (I Chron. 21:1 cf. I Thess. 2:18). Satan is seen here resisting Joshua the representative of Jerusalem and its people. Satan's desire throughout the Bible has been to make God's people unfit to be utilized by Him. He does this by corrupting the people of God, making them a reproach to the righteousness of God, and thereby worthy of wrath and judgment. In doing this Satan's desire is that God could not fulfill His plans to utilize his people to fulfill his will in the earth. Thus, Satan is standing at Joshua's right hand to resist him.

However the LORD rebukes Satan for this arrogant miscalculation of the eternal purpose of God with a resounding, "the LORD that hath chosen Jerusalem rebuke thee: is not this a brand plucked out of the fire?" With these words come the rebuke to Satan that God has a master plan for dealing with Israel's sin, so they as a nation can once again be utilized for God's intended purpose.

Filthy Garments (3-5): Joshua's filthy garments are a representation of what the nation had become. The mere fact that they had just come out of Babylonian captivity would attest to this fact. The LORD however is not taken back by the filthiness of His nation, but rather has a plan for dealing with the iniquity of the land and its people. The symbolic act of the LORD commanding those that stood by to take off the garments of Joshua testify to this reality, for the LORD goes on to say, "Behold I have caused thine iniquity to pass from thee..." (4).

Cleansing of the Nation (6-10): The angel of the LORD protests to Joshua regarding his manner of conduct and associated rewards to him for obedience (6-7). Then the angel of the LORD goes on to deal with events surrounding the removing of the iniquity of the land and its people. This national removal of sin will transpire when the LORD will bring forth His "BRANCH", the LORD Jesus Christ (Isa. 4:2, 60:21; Jer. 33:15; Ezek. 36:25; Zech. 6:12). This title is representative of the LORD Jesus Christ "planted" in the Kingdom (Isaiah 60:21). The establishment of the Theocratic Kingdom is the context of these verses. Thus, in verse 9 the stone that is engraved with seven eyes. The stone is representative of the stone that smites Daniels image, i.e. the LORD'S Kingdom subduing all other nations (Daniel 2:44-45). The seven eyes engraved on the stone are the seven spirits of God that will be utilized to bring about the occupation of the LORD'S Kingdom over the earth (vs. 9 cf. Rev. 5:6). All these highly visionary references are associated with the removal of the sins of the nation of Israel and is the main focus and theme of all things in this chapter:

"… and I will remove the iniquity of that land in one day. In that day, saith the LORD of hosts, shall ye call every man his neighbor under the vine and under the fig tree." (9-10).

Every man under his vine and under his fig tree is also a reference to the established Theocratic Kingdom; for once that kingdom is established the Feast of Tabernacles will be celebrated of which this is a reference (Zech. 14:6; Micah 4:4 cf. John 1:48 see I Kings 4:25 also).

Joshua the High Priest and the Cleansing of the Nation

OVERVIEW

- The Cleansing of the people and the land of Israel is what is in view. God's people had become spiritually unclean from their years of idolatry and their seventy years of Babylonian captivity. This uncleanliness is depicted by Joshua the high priest standing in filthy garment. Satan was the one who was intricately involved in corrupting God's people. His boasting is seen as he is standing at the right hand of Joshua before the angel of the LORD.

- "The LORD rebuke thee O Satan" is the answer from the angel of the LORD. The answer to Satan's boastfulness is that the LORD Himself will yet, "choose Jerusalem" for they are a "brand plucked from the fire". The LORD is not taken off guard by Satan's tactics, but rather has a plan to cleanse His people and the land, in the day when the BRANCH will come.

- The reality of the LORD "cleansing" His people and land is seen by the command by the angel of the LORD to have Joshua's filthy garments removed, placing clean garments upon him and a fair mitre. The angel of the LORD say emphatically, "Behold I have caused thine iniquity to pass from thee…".

- Joshua is given a warning to walk in the LORD's ways and keep the LORD's charge and in so doing Joshua will judge His house and keep His courts. This "protest" is for Joshua historically to obey the commandments of the LORD and he would fulfill his role as minister in the house of the LORD.

- The inability to walk after the Laws of God is seen in the need for the BRANCH to come. The stone representing the establishment of the LORD's Kingdom (Daniel's image) is seen laid before Joshua. This stone having seven eyes carved on it represents the seven spirits of God, instruments utilized by our LORD to bring about the removal of iniquity of Israel and the land.

- The removal of the iniquity of the people and the land will happen in one day, the LORD's Day. It will be at the time when all Israel will sit under the vine and under the fig tree; a reference to the coming Feast of Tabernacles which the Nation will celebrate once the Kingdom is established (see Zechariah 14:6).

CHAPTER FOUR

Not By Might, Nor By Power, But By My Spirit

And the angel that talked with me came again, and waked me, as a man that is wakened out of his sleep, And said unto me, What seest thou? And I said, I have looked, and behold a candlestick all of gold, with a bowl upon the top of it, and his seven lamps thereon, and seven pipes to the seven lamps, which are upon the top thereof: And two olive trees by it, one upon the right side of the bowl, and the other upon the left side thereof. So I answered and spake to the angel that talked with me, saying, What are these, my lord? Then the angel that talked with me answered and said unto me, Knowest thou not what these be? And I said, No, my lord. Then he answered and spake unto me, saying, This is the word of the LORD unto Zerubbabel, saying, Not by might, nor by power, but by my spirit, saith the LORD of hosts. Who art thou, O great mountain? before Zerubbabel thou shalt become a plain: and he shall bring forth the headstone thereof with shoutings, crying, Grace, grace unto it. Moreover the word of the LORD came unto me, saying, The hands of Zerubbabel have laid the foundation of this house; his hands shall also finish it; and thou shalt know that the LORD of hosts hath sent me unto you. For who hath despised the day of small things? for they shall rejoice, and shall see the plummet in the hand of Zerubbabel with those seven; they are the eyes of the LORD, which run to and fro through the whole earth. Then answered I, and said unto him, What are these two olive trees upon the right side of the candlestick and upon the left side thereof? And I answered again, and said unto him, What be these two olive branches which through the two golden pipes empty the golden oil out of themselves? And he answered me and said, Knowest thou not what these be? And I said, No, my lord. Then said he, These are the two anointed ones, that stand by the Lord of the whole earth. (Zechariah 4:1-14)

The Candlestick of the LORD (1-10): The main verse that sets the overall theme of this chapter is vs. 6, "...Not by might, nor by power, but by my spirit, saith the LORD of host." The vision of this chapter lays emphasis to this fact. The historical context is rebuilding the Temple, the house of the LORD. Zerubbabel (mentioned) in this chapter and Joshua (mentioned in the previous chapter) are the two involved in seeing the work to its completion. The promise to Zerubbabel is, "The hands of Zerubbabel have laid the foundation of this house: his hands shall also finish it..." (9); historically this did take place in four short years as a result of the prophesying of Haggai and Zechariah (Ezra 6:14, 15). However, this chapter (as we have pointed out in the previous chapters) looks far beyond the historical building of the Temple to a coming Temple that will be built.

The Vision of the Candlestick (1-3): The vision is that of a Menorah (candlestick) which has seven branches, each branch having seven lamps. Typically it was the priest's duty to keep the oil in the lamp, however above the candlestick is a bowl which has seven pipes feeding the oil to the seven lamps. On either side of the candlestick is an olive tree with two golden pipes going from the olive trees to the bowl above the candlestick, supplying oil through the seven golden pipes to the seven branches of the candlestick (see image).

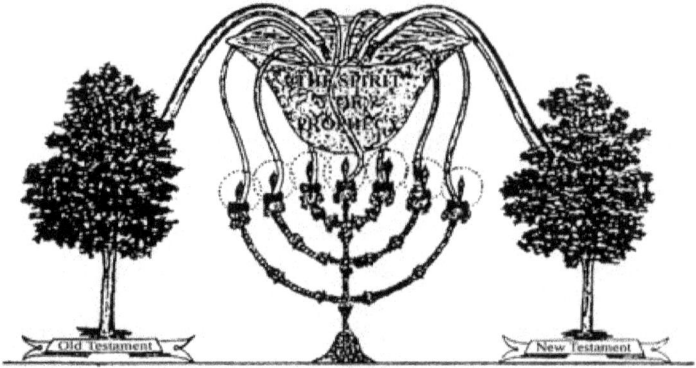

The overall purpose of the vision is to encourage Zerubbabel (6), by informing him that it is by the Spirit of the LORD (6) that he will complete the building of the Temple (9, 10). The candlestick is representative of Zerubbabel[6], he like the vision of the candlestick is being empowered by the oil from the two olive trees lightening the seven flames which are the seven spirits of the LORD (10). Like the candlestick, Zerubbabel is going to do the work he was created for, not by might, nor by power (his own) but by the spirit of the LORD (6 cf. 10, 12).

The Two Olive Trees (11-14): The Two Olive Trees are those who are being used to supply the oil to the candlestick; that makes the candlestick able to fulfill its purpose. Thus, the Two Olive Trees are the two prophets of the LORD who prophesy to Zerubbabel

---

[6] To have a person represented by the candlestick is not contrary to Scripture, it is used in Revelation 11:3-4 to represent the LORD's two witnesses.

stirring up his spirit, motivating him to complete the work of the LORD:

Then Zerubbabel the son of Shealtiel, and Joshua the son of Josedech, the high priest, with all the remnant of the people, obeyed the voice of the LORD their God, and the <u>words of Haggai the prophet</u>, as the LORD their God had sent him, and the people did fear before the LORD. Then spake Haggai the LORD'S messenger in the LORD'S message unto the people, saying, I am with you, saith the LORD. And the LORD <u>stirred up the spirit of Zerubbabel</u> the son of Shealtiel, governor of Judah, and the <u>spirit of Joshua</u> the son of Josedech, the high priest, and <u>the spirit of all the remnant</u> of the people; and they came and did work in the house of the LORD of hosts, their God, (Haggai 1:12-14)

And the elders of the Jews builded, and they prospered through the prophesying of Haggai the prophet and Zechariah the son of Iddo. And they builded, and finished it, according to the commandment of the God of Israel, and according to the commandment of Cyrus, and Darius, and Artaxerxes king of Persia. And this house was finished on the third day of the month Adar, which was in the sixth year of the reign of Darius the king. (Ezra 6:14-15)

Thus, by the prophesying of Haggai and Zechariah the Temple is completed in four short years. These are the LORD's two witnesses at the time of Zerubbabel.[7] They are the two anointed ones that stand before the LORD of the whole earth, fulfilling His will. They empty themselves by their prophesying, moving Zerubbabel, Joshua and the people to see the work of the Temple is completed.

The Mountain, the Plain and the Headstone (7): The mountain is representative of all the various obstacles that Zerubbabel is encountering trying to build the Temple. They are obstructing him from completing his task. The LORD however is continuing the encouraging words to Zerubbabel by telling him that the mountain of resistance will be removed from obstructing you, it will become a plain and then you will place the headstone, the finishing stone i.e. "... his hands shall also finish it..." (9). The shouting of joy was heard at the laying of the foundation (Ezra 3:10-13) and the voice of shouting will be heard at its completion (7).

---

[7] It is thought that the two witnesses in Revelation 11:3-4 are the same as these Two Olive Trees. However, historically the Two Olive Trees at the time of Zerubbabel are Haggai and Zechariah. The LORD has another two witnesses that will stand before the LORD of all the earth in the future, fulfilling their role on the earth as Haggai and Zechariah were called to do. The olive trees in the future will be Moses and Elijah.

The Day of Small Things (10): When the Temple foundation was laid the people rejoiced (Ezra 3:10-11), however the ancients of the people who had seen Solomon's Temple wept with a loud voice (Ezra 3:12). These are they who despised the day of small things. The LORD will see to it however that these men that despise the day of small things shall, "... see the plummet in the hand of Zerubbabel" (10).

The Seven Lamps and the Eyes of the LORD (3, 10): The seven lamps are the seven spirits of God:

John to the seven churches which are in Asia: Grace be unto you, and peace, from him which is, and which was, and which is to come; and from the seven Spirits which are before his throne; (Revelation 1:4)

And unto the angel of the church in Sardis write; These things saith he that hath the seven Spirits of God, and the seven stars; I know thy works, that thou hast a name that thou livest, and art dead. (Revelation 3:1)

And out of the throne proceeded lightnings and thunderings and voices: and there were seven lamps of fire burning before the throne, which are the seven Spirits of God. (Revelation 4:5)

And I beheld, and, lo, in the midst of the throne and of the four beasts, and in the midst of the elders, stood a Lamb as it had been slain, having seven horns and seven eyes, which are the seven Spirits of God sent forth into all the earth. (Revelation 5:6)

The purpose and function of these Seven Spirits of the LORD is not clearly seen, however they are seen before the LORD, they are at His disposal and seem to play a role in the LORD's reclaiming the earth and establishment of His kingdom.

Not By Might, Nor By Power, But By My Spirit

OVERVIEW

- The vision in this chapter is of two olive trees that have oil flow from them through a golden pipe to a golden bowl; from the golden bowl the oil flows through seven golden pipes to the seven branches of a candlestick. This vision represents people and events surrounding the historical setting of the book of Zechariah.

- The vision of chapter four is regarding Zerubbabel (6), he is the emphasis throughout this chapter (6, 7, 9, and 10). He is the one, with Joshua the high priest (dealt with in chapter three) that is being encouraged to complete the work of building the temple that was started. The foundation was laid in two short years, but through adversaries in the land the foundation sat vacant for over fourteen years.

- Zerubbabel is told that not only did he lay the foundation, but he will build the temple as well; he will see it to completion (9). The building of the temple however will not be done by any personal might or power on the part of Zerubbabel but by the spirit of the LORD (6).

- The direction and motivation to do the work of the LORD will flow from the ministries of two men, Haggai and Zechariah (12, 14). They are the ones who stand for the LORD of the whole earth, the spokesmen of the LORD (14).

CHAPTER FIVE
Wickedness

Then I turned, and lifted up mine eyes, and looked, and behold a flying roll. And he said unto me, What seest thou? And I answered, I see a flying roll; the length thereof is twenty cubits, and the breadth thereof ten cubits. Then said he unto me, This is the curse that goeth forth over the face of the whole earth: for every one that stealeth shall be cut off as on this side according to it; and every one that sweareth shall be cut off as on that side according to it. I will bring it forth, saith the LORD of hosts, and it shall enter into the house of the thief, and into the house of him that sweareth falsely by my name: and it shall remain in the midst of his house, and shall consume it with the timber thereof and the stones thereof. (Zechariah 5:1-4)

A Flying Scroll (1-4): The flying scroll is a roll of a book with curses in it much like that of Jeremiah 36 and that of Ezekiel 2 & 3. One of the most peculiar aspects of the scroll is its size, twenty cubits (30 feet) by ten Cubits (15 feet). This is the identical size of the *Holy Place*, the room before the *Holy of Holies* in the Temple and Tabernacle (Exodus 26:33). Two specific sins are mentioned in this section: Those that steal and those that swear falsely; thus the curse shall enter the house of the **thief** and the house of him that **sweareth false by My Name** (4). The remnant of Jews that returned from their Babylonian captivity did so with the trappings of 70 years of not having a place of worship. Thus, they are expected to learn from their sins of the past (See Zechariah 7). The LORD will not overlook their transgressions: the house that sinneth will be judged (4).

The following vision is going to deal with the issue of removing these lingering sins and the influence of Babylon. It is also looking forward to the time when the LORD will remove the sins from the land and His people for good (3:9).

Then the angel that talked with me went forth, and said unto me, Lift up now thine eyes, and see what is this that goeth forth. And I said, What is it? And

he said, This is an ephah that goeth forth. He said moreover, This is their resemblance through all the earth. And, behold, there was lifted up a talent of lead: and this is a woman that sitteth in the midst of the ephah. And he said, This is wickedness. And he cast it into the midst of the ephah; and he cast the weight of lead upon the mouth thereof. Then lifted I up mine eyes, and looked, and, behold, there came out two women, and the wind was in their wings; for they had wings like the wings of a stork: and they lifted up the ephah between the earth and the heaven. Then said I to the angel that talked with me, Whither do these bear the ephah? And he said unto me, To build it an house in the land of Shinar: and it shall be established, and set there upon her own base. (Zechariah 5:5-11)

The Rise of Babylon (5-11): Interpreting this section is not without its difficulty. However, the symbolism used in the vision gives us clues as to a possible understanding of the vision:

- **An Ephah** in this context is the instrument used in measuring out an Ephah (the dry measurement of about a bushel) most likely a basket. It has to do with commerce, merchants and merchandise.
- **A Woman representing wickedness** is seen in the Ephah. We will be able to get a better

understanding of this once we understand where she is going.

- **Lead** is used to keep the wickedness in the Ephah for its journey.
- **Two women with wings of a stork** carry off the Ephah. A stork is an unclean bird (Lev. 11:13-19) which would be fitting considering they are responsible for transporting the Ephah of wickedness. In the Bible angels do not have wings; angelic creatures have wings (Seraphim and Cherubim) and devils have wings (Matt. 13:4, 19, 31-32).
- **The land of Shinar,** is Babylon (Gen. 10:10, 11:1-2; Dan. 1:1-2).
- **To build a house, to establish it on a base.** The goal is to "establish" wickedness back in the land of Shinar.

As was mentioned in the previous verses, the issue of removing the sinful influence of Babylon is in view. However, with the removing of this sinfulness or "wickedness" from the land and sending it back to its place of origin, there is a great underlying truth to this vison we need to understand. Before we put all this together, we need to familiarize ourselves with the truth that though Babylon has fallen historically, the Bible makes it clear that it will rise again one day. It will become the center for all world trade in the region. The fall of this future Babylon is taught throughout Scripture but most notably in Isaiah 13-14, Jeremiah 50-51 and in Revelation 17-18:

And Babylon, the glory of kingdoms, the beauty of the Chaldees' excellency, shall be as when God overthrew Sodom and Gomorrah. It shall never be inhabited, neither shall it be dwelt in from generation to generation: neither shall the Arabian pitch tent there; neither shall the shepherds make their fold there. But wild beasts of the desert shall lie there; and their houses shall be full of doleful creatures; and owls shall dwell there, and satyrs shall dance there. And the wild beasts of the islands shall cry in their desolate houses, and dragons in their pleasant palaces: and her time is near to come, and her days shall not be prolonged. (Isaiah 13:19-22)

Therefore the wild beasts of the desert with the wild beasts of the islands shall dwell there, and the owls shall dwell therein: and it shall be no more inhabited for ever; neither shall it be dwelt in from generation to generation. As God overthrew Sodom and Gomorrah and the neighbour cities thereof, saith the LORD; so shall no man abide there, neither shall any son of man dwell therein. (Jeremiah 50:39-40)

For all nations have drunk of the wine of the wrath of her fornication, and the kings of the earth have committed fornication with her, and the merchants of the earth are waxed rich through the abundance of her delicacies. (Revelation 18:3)

And the merchants of the earth shall weep and mourn over her; for no man buyeth their merchandise any more: The merchandise of gold, and silver, and precious stones, and of pearls, and fine linen, and purple, and silk, and scarlet, and all thyine wood, and all manner vessels of ivory, and all manner vessels of most precious wood, and of brass, and iron, and marble, And cinnamon, and odours, and ointments, and frankincense, and wine, and oil, and fine flour, and wheat, and beasts, and sheep, and horses, and chariots, and slaves, and souls of men. And the fruits that thy soul lusted after are departed from thee, and all things which were dainty and goodly are departed from thee, and thou shalt find them no more at all. The merchants of these things, which were made rich by her, shall stand afar off for the fear of her torment, weeping and wailing, (Revelation 18:11-15)

In these verses (and these chapters) you have the destruction of Babylon. This is not just simply "mystery" Babylon; that is, these chapters are not just dealing with spiritual idolatry or a false religious system. Though it is true that all idolatry comes from Babylon and that all false religions can find their roots in Babylon, these chapters are clearly a prophetic announcement of a future fall of a literal city of Babylon.

Therefore, because there is a future **fall** of Babylon there has to be a future **rebuilding** of that city. Babylon today is far from what is depicted in Revelation 17 & 18. Therefore, the future rise of Babylon has to take place. It will have to rise to such powers that not only is it called "that Great City" but when it does fall all the **merchants of the earth** that trade with it will weep and mourn over its fall.[8]

It is, therefore, this future rise to power that is hinted at in this vision given to Zechariah.

The Interpretation of the Vision: The vision is regarding removing the wickedness of the land and people of God. This wickedness is seen in the woman in the Ephah and the women with wings of a stork (unclean bird) that carry it to the land of Shinar, the land of Babylon (unclean place).

---

[8] Saddam Husain's desire was to rebuild Babylon to its past glory. He spent almost 20 years, hundreds of millions of dollars and over some 60 million bricks in attempts to rebuild Babylon. The city of Babylon being rebuilt by Saddam, included Nebuchadnezzar's throne room, the Ishtar Gate, the Processional Way, the Ninmakh Temple and the Ishtar Temple, all which saw completion before his capture and death.

However, the underlying truth is that Babylon will be rebuilt and become that seat of all wickedness in the future. I believe that these verses give us an insight to the future rise of Babylon.

- The Ephah with the women of wickedness is placed in Shinar in the land of Babylon; it is Babylon that is the seat of all wickedness (Rev. 17:5)

- This vision is a woman of wickedness; this would be likened to the woman in Revelation 17 &18 which is Babylon (Rev. 17:1, 18 cf. 18:2, 16-21).

- This vision deals with measurements (she is placed in an Ephah), which is commerce. When Babylon is destroyed in Revelation 18 all the "merchants" weep and mourn (Rev. 18:3, 11, 15, 23 cf. Rev. 18:12-14).

- The purpose in bringing the Ephah of wickedness is to "**build it a house** in the land of Shinar; and it shall be **established** and set there upon **her own base**" (11). It is this verse specifically that I believe gives us the insight into the re-establishment of Babylon as a world power. Thus, how does Babylon get to the place of power and influence that we see in the book of Revelation? This vision and this verse gives us that answer.

Wickedness

OVERVIEW

- The vision is dealing with the judgment and removal of sin from the LORD's land and people. The Jewish people were influenced by Babylon, having come out of 70 years of Babylonian Captivity. It is this influence that is the issue in this vision both historically and prophetically.

- The curse that goes forth over the face of the whole earth is the Law that will judge the house of those who stealeth and those who sweareth falsely, they obey not the Law of the LORD. The vision also hints at the reality that the LORD will remove all iniquity of the land and people in "a day" (3:10).

- The wickedness of the land is dealing with commerce which is seen by the vision of the Ephah and the women of wickedness placed therein. This is seen in Revelation 18 and the influence that Babylon has over all the "merchants" of the earth.

- This vision also carries with it the reality that a future Babylon will be established as the world power in the land of Shinar, Babylon.

The Ephah is placed in Shinar to "build it a house" to "establish it" and "set it upon her own base" (5:11).

CHAPTER SIX
The Coming BRANCH

And I turned, and lifted up mine eyes, and looked, and, behold, there came four chariots out from between two mountains; and the mountains were mountains of brass. In the first chariot were red horses; and in the second chariot black horses; And in the third chariot white horses; and in the fourth chariot grisled and bay horses. Then I answered and said unto the angel that talked with me, What are these, my lord? And the angel answered and said unto me, These are the four spirits of the heavens, which go forth from standing before the Lord of all the earth. The black horses which are therein go forth into the north country; and the white go forth after them; and the grisled go forth toward the south country. And the bay went forth, and sought to go that they might walk to and fro through the earth: and he said, Get you hence, walk to and fro through the earth. So they walked to and fro through the earth. Then cried he upon me, and spake unto me, saying, Behold, these that go toward the north country have quieted my spirit in the north country. (Zechariah 6:1-8)

The Chariots of God's Judgment (1-8): This is the last of the visions of Zechariah. The interpretation of these visions have been very challenging to say the least. One only need to read a few commentators' remarks to see the interpretations are anything but congruent. So while I will give you my understanding of these final visions, I understand perfectly well that other interpretations are not without merit or worthy of consideration.

Before looking into these final visions we need to remind ourselves once again how the LORD records prophecy in His Word. The LORD will place prophetical messages within passages dealing with similar events. Historically, in Zechariah's time, the Jewish people are coming out of Babylon and rebuilding the Temple. Thus, the LORD has placed in these passages prophetic scriptures that deal with a similar event in the future; a time when the LORD will call His people of out Babylon, destroy it and establish His Temple. It is these events that have been, and will continue to be, the focus of Zechariah.

Before interpreting this first vision we will make some general comments on the chariots and mountains of brass.

The Four Chariots: Chariots are part of the heavenly realm and speak of the judgment of the LORD (2 Kings 6:17 cf. Psalm 68:17). These chariots will be utilized when the LORD comes to reclaim the earth, avenge Israel and establish His Kingdom (Isaiah

66:15 cf. Hab. 3:8). These chariots are four in number because they go in the four directions of the earth (though only north and south are mentioned, the other points are assumed, for the four chariots "walk to and fro through the earth"). These chariots are said to be the "four spirits of the heavens" (5). Thus, they are His angelic army, at His disposal. The color of the horses are significant, and speak to the judgments of the four horses of the Apocalypse. An interesting note: The word for chariot is *Merkabah*, this same word is used by Israel for its brand of tanks.

The Merkava 4, the main battle tank in Israe,l takes its name from the Hebrew word for chariot.

The Two Mountains of Brass: Mountains in the Bible are sometimes likened to Kingdoms (Daniel 2:45; Rev. 17:9) or they could be literal mountains (Zech. 14:4). If literal, the mountains mentioned here would be Mount Zion and the Mount of Olives. However, if they are literal mountains, why the reference to brass? Brass often symbolizes judgment: The Altar of Sacrifice in the Temple was covered in brass, the serpent that Moses put on the pole was made of brass.

To understand the vision of the four chariots that come between two mountains of brass, we need to look at this in light of the vision of chapter one; the horses among the myrtle trees.

In chapter one the horses come from "walking to and fro through the earth" (1:11) just as these chariots have (6:7). In the first vision in chapter one, the horses give the report that all the world is at rest (1:11). This report is met with a cry from the angel of the LORD saying, "O LORD of hosts, how long wilt thou not have mercy on Jerusalem and on the cities of Judah..." (1:12). What follows in the remainder of Zechariah chapter one is the "comforting words" regarding the mercy the LORD will show toward Jerusalem. So then the horsemen that report the earth is at rest are reporting this as a negative. The earth is at rest while the people of God suffer.

In the chariot vision of this chapter, the chariots go throughout the earth (6:6-7) and bring back report, however only the chariot from the north country gives a report that quieted the angel's spirit (5:7-8). It is the quieting the angel's spirit that gives insight to this vision. In the first vision the angel's spirit was **NOT** quieted, in fact it cried out to the LORD regarding the earth being at rest while God's people suffer (6:12). Now notice the response of the angel once he receives the report from the north: "…These that go toward the north country **HAVE** quieted my spirit in the north country." The angel's spirit is "quieted" because the Gentiles are **NOT** at rest in the north; God is judging the countries of the north. There is judgment befalling these Gentile nations that God's people are subservient to. It is therefore the report of judgment befalling the Gentile nations that "quieted" the angel's spirit. As to which Gentile nation is represented by the two mountains of brass, we need to remind ourselves who is the dominant world power at the time of Zechariah. The world power at the time of Zechariah is the Medo-Persia Empire, and following them will be the Grecian Empire. These Gentile powers are all foretold in the book of Daniel:

Thou, O king, sawest, and behold a great image. This great image, whose brightness was excellent, stood before thee; and the form thereof was terrible. This image's head was of fine gold, his breast and his arms of silver, <u>his belly and his thighs of brass</u>, His legs of iron, his feet part of iron and part of clay. Thou sawest till that a stone

was cut out without hands, which smote the image upon his feet that were of iron and clay, and brake them to pieces. (Daniel 2:31-34)

Thou, O king, art a king of kings: for the God of heaven hath given thee a kingdom, power, and strength, and glory. And wheresoever the children of men dwell, the beasts of the field and the fowls of the heaven hath he given into thine hand, and hath made thee ruler over them all. Thou art this head of gold. And after thee shall arise another kingdom inferior to thee, and <u>another third kingdom of brass</u>, which shall bear rule over all the earth. (Daniel 2:37-39)

In Daniel's image, Nebuchadnezzar's kingdom is represented by the head of gold. The arms and breast of silver are the Medo-Persian Empire, and the belly and thighs of brass are the Grecian Empire, with the iron and clay to follow. The last Kingdom will be the LORD's; it is represented by the stone cut without hands that topples all other kingdoms of the world. Notice that the Grecian Empire is represented by brass. This is the empire that will topple the Medo-Persian Empire. Therefore, the coming war between these two powers is the subject of this vison of the chariots coming between two mountains of brass.

And the word of the LORD came unto me, saying, Take of them of the captivity, even of Heldai, of Tobijah, and of Jedaiah, which are come from Babylon, and come thou the same day, and go into the house of Josiah the son of Zephaniah; Then take silver and gold, and make crowns, and set them upon the head of Joshua the son of Josedech, the high priest; And speak unto him, saying, Thus speaketh the LORD of hosts, saying, Behold the man whose name is The BRANCH; and he shall grow up out of his place, and he shall build the temple of the LORD: Even he shall build the temple of the LORD; and he shall bear the glory, and shall sit and rule upon his throne; and he shall be a priest upon his throne: and the counsel of peace shall be between them both. And the crowns shall be to Helem, and to Tobijah, and to Jedaiah, and to Hen the son of Zephaniah, for a memorial in the temple of the LORD. And they that are far off shall come and build in the temple of the LORD, and ye shall know that the LORD of hosts hath sent me unto you. And this shall come to pass, if ye will diligently obey the voice of the LORD your God. (Zechariah 6:9-15)

The Symbolic Act that has a Prophetic Fulfillment (9-15): Zechariah is told to do something at the time of the rebuilding of the Temple that looks out to a future day when the LORD will come and sit in His Temple and rule all nations.

73

Zechariah is to go to the house of Josiah where Heldai, Tobijah, and Jedaiah, which are come from Babylon, dwelt. Having the material goods required for this task, he is to take silver and gold to make crowns and place them on the head of Joshua, the son of Josedech, the high priest (10-11).

Once this is done, he is to speak unto him saying, "Thus, speaketh the LORD of hosts, saying, Behold the man whose name is The BRANCH; and he shall grow up out of his place, and he shall build the temple of the LORD. Even he shall build the temple of the LORD and he shall bear the glory, and shall sit and rule upon his throne and he shall be a priest upon his throne: and the counsel of peace shall be between them both." (12-13). This symbolic act is followed by the placing of the crowns in the Temple of the LORD by Helem, Tobijah and Jedaiah for a "memorial" of what was said the crowns represented (14 cf. 12-13). The LORD is the BRANCH (Jer. 23:5, 33:15; Zech. 3:8); as is stated in chapter three of Zechariah, this title looks to a day when He will be "planted" in His Kingdom on the throne of David forever. The temple of the LORD at the time of Zechariah does get built, but the people do not "diligently obey the voice of the LORD ..." (15) and therefore the fulfilment of this awaits a future day, the time in which verses 12 & 13 describe.

This will end the visions of Zechariah.

The Coming BRANCH

OVERVIEW

- Zechariah sees four chariots, the spirits of the heavens sent forth in all the earth from the angel of the LORD, coming between two mountains of brass. The chariot from the north country brings a report that quieted his spirit. This quieting of the angel's spirit is the result of the report that the chariot of the north has brought back. The north country is not at rest in the report, Gentile nations are at war, thus God is fulfilling His judgment on the nations and getting closer to establishing His kingdom.

- The mountains of brass is the Grecian Empire that will come and overthrow the Medo-Persian Empire. All these Gentile kingdoms are foretold in the book of Daniel (Dan. 2). And all this looks forward to the day in which the God of Heaven will establish His Kingdom in the earth.

- Zechariah then is told to do a symbolic act of crowning Joshua the high priest with crowns of gold and silver. Zechariah then makes a prophetic announcement regarding the coming BRANCH that will come and sit on His throne and rule as both Priest and King. This is the LORD Jesus Christ who will come and be planted in His Kingdom forever.

- Then the crowns are to be placed in the Temple for a memorial of this prophetic announcement of a coming Priest and King, the BRANCH of Israel, the LORD Jesus Christ.

CHAPTER SEVEN
Fasting Versus Feasting

And it came to pass in the fourth year of king Darius, that the word of the LORD came unto Zechariah in the fourth day of the ninth month, even in Chisleu; When they had sent unto the house of God Sherezer and Regemmelech, and their men, to pray before the LORD, And to speak unto the priests which were in the house of the LORD of hosts, and to the prophets, saying, Should I weep in the fifth month, separating myself, as I have done these so many years? (Zechariah 7:1-3)

A Question of Tradition (1-3): The Jewish people had been given only one fast to observe according to the Law of Moses; it was on the annual Day of Atonement (Lev. 23:16-32). However, four new fasts were added to commemorate the destruction of Jerusalem and the Temple:

- Fast in the **tenth month** when the Babylonians had begun the siege on the city.
- Fast in the **fourth month**, when the city walls had been broken through.
- Fast in the **fifth month**, when the Temple was burned.
- Fast in the **seventh month**, when the governor Gedaliah had been assassinated (see Zech. 8:19).

It was with regard to these added fasts that Sherezer and Regemmelech are sent to the priests (3). Their questioning is along these lines, "Now that we are back in the land and are rebuilding our Temple, do we need to continue the added fasts surrounding the destruction of the Temple?" The specific question is regarding the fifth fast which was to commemorate the burning of the Temple.

Then came the word of the LORD of hosts unto me, saying, Speak unto all the people of the land, and to the priests, saying, When ye fasted and mourned in the fifth and seventh month, even those seventy years, did ye at all fast unto me, even to me? And when ye did eat, and when ye did drink, did not ye eat for yourselves, and drink for yourselves? Should ye not hear the words which the LORD hath cried by the former prophets, when Jerusalem was inhabited and in prosperity, and the

cities thereof round about her, when men inhabited the south and the plain? (Zechariah 7:4-7)

A Question of the Heart (4-7): Zechariah does not answer their question directly, but answers it with a question (see our Lord Mark 11:27-33). The question back to those inquiring about the fasts is, "When ye fasted and mourned in the fifth and the seventh month, even those seventy years, did ye at all fast unto me, even to me?" The issue being brought out by this question is: did they fast merely as a form a traditionalism or was it from the heart toward God? The Jewish people have stumbled continually over this very issue. They would keep the formalism of the service of the Temple, while in their personal experiences they would be far removed. Going all the way back to the times of Samuel, the LORD had told them that to obey was better than sacrifice (I Sam. 15:22). They were even warned by the prophets of God, prior to their Babylonian captivity, of this very issue (vs. 7). When our LORD was on earth, He warned the religious leaders of this hypocritical behavior (Mark 7:1-23). Even the future Remnant of the LORD will be reminded of this subject (James 1:27; 2). This behavior is still very prevalent in the lives of the Jewish people in Zechariah's time, even following 70 years of judgment.

And the word of the LORD came unto Zechariah, saying, Thus speaketh the LORD of hosts, saying, Execute true judgment, and shew mercy and compassions every man to his brother: And oppress not the widow, nor the fatherless, the stranger, nor the poor; and let none of you imagine evil against his brother in your heart. But they refused to hearken, and pulled away the shoulder, and stopped their ears, that they should not hear. Yea, they made their hearts as an adamant stone, lest they should hear the law, and the words which the LORD of hosts hath sent in his spirit by the former prophets: therefore came a great wrath from the LORD of hosts. Therefore it is come to pass, that as he cried, and they would not hear; so they cried, and I would not hear, saith the LORD of hosts: But I scattered them with a whirlwind among all the nations whom they knew not. Thus the land was desolate after them, that no man passed through nor returned: for they laid the pleasant land desolate. (Zechariah 7:8-14)

The Hard Heart of Israel (8-14): Through Zechariah the LORD reminds His people that it was the vain religion of their fathers that caused them to be scattered among the nations (13-14). The warnings to this remnant coming out of 70 years of Babylonian influence is to have a change of heart, to obey the Law of the LORD from the heart (8-10). The religious leaders do not harken, and by the time our

LORD is here on earth these leaders are entrenched in a false religious system:

This people draweth nigh unto me with their mouth, and honoureth me with their lips; but their heart is far from me. But in vain they do worship me, teaching for doctrines the commandments of men. (Matthew 15:8-9)

Woe unto you, scribes and Pharisees, hypocrites! for ye devour widows' houses, and for a pretence make long prayer: therefore ye shall receive the greater damnation. (Matthew 23:14)

The scattering of the Jewish people "among the nations" is a reference to Jerusalem's final destruction and the deportation of the Jews into captivity of Babylon. The reason for this "scattering" is not adhering to the prophets of the LORD:

Wherefore ye be witnesses unto yourselves, that ye are the children of them which killed the prophets. Fill ye up then the measure of your fathers. (Matthew 23:31-32)

Thus, the "pleasant land" (see Daniel 11:16, 41) was laid waste. The warning is clear; they need to listen and obey the voice of the prophets, lest the "pleasant land" be laid waste in judgment again (see Zech. 14:2).

CHAPTER EIGHT
The LORD's Desire for Zion

Again the word of the LORD of hosts came to me, saying, Thus saith the LORD of hosts; I was jealous for Zion with great jealousy, and I was jealous for her with great fury. Thus saith the LORD; I am returned unto Zion, and will dwell in the midst of Jerusalem: and Jerusalem shall be called a city of truth; and the mountain of the LORD of hosts the holy mountain. Thus saith the LORD of hosts; There shall yet old men and old women dwell in the streets of Jerusalem, and every man with his staff in his hand for very age. And the streets of the city shall be full of boys and girls playing in the streets thereof. Thus saith the LORD of hosts; If it be marvellous in the eyes of the remnant of this people in these days, should it also be marvellous in mine eyes? saith the LORD of hosts. Thus saith the LORD of hosts; Behold, I will save my people from the east country, and from the west country; And I will bring them, and they shall dwell in the midst of Jerusalem: and they shall be my people, and I will be their God, in truth and in righteousness. (Zechariah 8:1-8)

The Future of Zion (1-8): This chapter is a continuation of the previous; where chapter seven left off with the warning of future scattering, this chapter promises that the LORD will "return unto Zion and dwell in the midst of Jerusalem." This is the promise to the people of God throughout the prophets, and therefore, any who try and spiritualize it away are in great error. Notice the very descriptive details concerning this future time:

- There shall yet old men and old women dwell in the streets of Jerusalem
- The streets of the city shall be full of young boys and girls
- They shall play in the streets
- They shall dwell in the midst of Jerusalem

It is this future establishment of the LORD's Kingdom in Jerusalem that is the consistent hope of Israel, not only in Zechariah but all throughout the Scriptures.

Thus saith the LORD of hosts; Let your hands be strong, ye that hear in these days these words by the mouth of the prophets, which were in the day that the foundation of the house of the LORD of hosts was laid, that the temple might be built. For before these days there was no hire for man, nor any hire for beast; neither was there any peace to him that went out or came in because of the affliction: for I set all men every one against his

neighbour. But now I will not be unto the residue of this people as in the former days, saith the LORD of hosts. For the seed shall be prosperous; the vine shall give her fruit, and the ground shall give her increase, and the heavens shall give their dew; and I will cause the remnant of this people to possess all these things. And it shall come to pass, that as ye were a curse among the heathen, O house of Judah, and house of Israel; so will I save you, and ye shall be a blessing: fear not, but let your hands be strong. For thus saith the LORD of hosts; As I thought to punish you, when your fathers provoked me to wrath, saith the LORD of hosts, and I repented not: So again have I thought in these days to do well unto Jerusalem and to the house of Judah: fear ye not. These are the things that ye shall do; Speak ye every man the truth to his neighbour; execute the judgment of truth and peace in your gates: And let none of you imagine evil in your hearts against his neighbour; and love no false oath: for all these are things that I hate, saith the LORD. (Zechariah 8:9-17)

Curses and Blessings (9-15): The LORD contrasts what Israel was to what it will be upon the establishment of the Kingdom. Because of Israel's disobedience they reaped the curse of the Law (See Duet. 11:26-32 cf. Lev. 26). The prophet Haggai, prophesying at the same time as Zechariah, mentions this judgment upon their prosperity:

Ye have sown much, and bring in little; ye eat, but ye have not enough; ye drink, but ye are not filled with drink; ye clothe you, but there is none warm; and he that earneth wages earneth wages to put it into a bag with holes. (Haggai 1:6)

Ye looked for much, and, lo, it came to little; and when ye brought it home, I did blow upon it. Why? saith the LORD of hosts. Because of mine house that is waste, and ye run every man unto his own house. (Haggai 1:9)

The LORD's covenant with Israel was based upon their performance of it. If they obeyed the laws of God, they would be "blessed" physically in the details of their lives:

And it shall come to pass, if thou shalt hearken diligently unto the voice of the LORD thy God, to observe and to do all his commandments which I command thee this day, that the LORD thy God will set thee on high above all nations of the earth: And all these blessings shall come on thee, and overtake thee, if thou shalt hearken unto the voice of the LORD thy God. Blessed shalt thou be in the city, and blessed shalt thou be in the field. Blessed shall be the fruit of thy body, and the fruit of thy ground, and the fruit of thy cattle, the increase of thy kine, and the flocks of thy sheep. Blessed shall be thy basket and thy store. Blessed shalt thou be when thou comest in, and blessed shalt thou be

when thou goest out. The LORD shall cause thine enemies that rise up against thee to be smitten before thy face: they shall come out against thee one way, and flee before thee seven ways. The LORD shall command the blessing upon thee in thy storehouses, and in all that thou settest thine hand unto; and he shall bless thee in the land which the LORD thy God giveth thee. The LORD shall establish thee an holy people unto himself, as he hath sworn unto thee, if thou shalt keep the commandments of the LORD thy God, and walk in his ways. (Deuteronomy 28:1-9)

However, if they refused to harken unto the words of the LORD, and turn from Him they would merit the "curses" of the law contract God made with them:

But it shall come to pass, if thou wilt not hearken unto the voice of the LORD thy God, to observe to do all his commandments and his statutes which I command thee this day; that all these curses shall come upon thee, and overtake thee: Cursed shalt thou be in the city, and cursed shalt thou be in the field. Cursed shall be thy basket and thy store. Cursed shall be the fruit of thy body, and the fruit of thy land, the increase of thy kine, and the flocks of thy sheep. Cursed shalt thou be when thou comest in, and cursed shalt thou be when thou goest out. The LORD shall send upon thee cursing, vexation, and rebuke, in all that thou settest thine hand unto for to do, until thou be destroyed, and until thou perish quickly; because of the wickedness of thy doings, whereby thou hast forsaken me. The LORD shall make the pestilence cleave unto thee, until he have consumed thee from off the land, whither thou goest to possess it. The LORD shall smite thee with a consumption, and with a fever, and with an inflammation, and with an extreme burning, and with the sword, and with blasting, and with mildew; and they shall pursue thee until thou perish. <u>And thy heaven that is over thy head shall be brass, and the earth that is under thee shall be iron. The LORD shall make the rain of thy land powder and dust: from heaven shall it come down upon thee, until thou be destroyed.</u> (Deuteronomy 28:15-24)

The sad history of the Jewish people is that of disobedience to the LORD. However, the LORD again shows His mercy in the continual offer to both Israel and Judah the blessings of the Law, if they will only harken to Him and walk in His ways (13-17).

And the word of the LORD of hosts came unto me, saying, Thus saith the LORD of hosts; The fast of the fourth month, and the fast of the fifth, and the fast of the seventh, and the fast of the tenth, shall be to the house of Judah joy and gladness, and cheerful feasts; therefore love the truth and peace. Thus saith the LORD of hosts; It shall yet come to pass, that there shall come people, and the inhabitants of many cities: And the inhabitants of one city shall go to another, saying, Let us go speedily to pray before the LORD, and to seek the LORD of hosts: I will go also. Yea, many people and strong nations shall come to seek the LORD of hosts in Jerusalem, and to pray before the LORD. Thus saith the LORD of hosts; In those days it shall come to pass, that ten men shall take hold out of all languages of the nations, even shall take hold of the skirt of him that is a Jew, saying, We will go with you: for we have heard that God is with you. (Zechariah 8:18-23)

Fasting to Feasting (18-23): In chapter seven the question was put forth whether the people should still observe fasts that were added in connection to the destruction of the city and the Temple:

- Fast in the **tenth month** when the Babylonians had begun the siege on the city
- Fast in the **fourth month**, when the city walls had been broken through
- Fast in the **fifth month**, when the Temple was burned
- Fast in the **seventh month**, when the governor Gedaliah had been assassinated

The LORD now answers this very question; the fasting will be turned into feasting:

And the word of the LORD of hosts came unto me, saying, Thus saith the LORD of hosts; The fast of the fourth month, and the fast of the fifth, and the fast of the seventh, and the fast of the tenth, <u>shall be to the house of Judah joy and gladness, and cheerful feasts;</u> therefore love the truth and peace. (Zechariah 8:18-19)

This most blessed event for God's people still waits its fulfillment. It will be at the time when God is with them, sitting in their midst (23). The picture in this chapter is the people and their city being the blessing to the rest of the world, which the Abrahamic Covenant called for. The LORD had intended His people and His Temple to be towards all people, to be the light to the Gentile world (Isa. 2:1-5; cf. 56:7; 60 cf. Matt. 21:13).

CHAPTER NINE
The Burden of the Word of the LORD

The burden of the word of the LORD in the land of Hadrach, and Damascus shall be the rest thereof: when the eyes of man, as of all the tribes of Israel, shall be toward the LORD. And Hamath also shall border thereby; Tyrus, and Zidon, though it be very wise. And Tyrus did build herself a strong hold, and heaped up silver as the dust, and fine gold as the mire of the streets. Behold, the Lord will cast her out, and he will smite her power in the sea; and she shall be devoured with fire. Ashkelon shall see it, and fear; Gaza also shall see it, and be very sorrowful, and Ekron; for her expectation shall be ashamed; and the king shall perish from Gaza, and Ashkelon shall not be inhabited. And a bastard shall dwell in Ashdod, and I will cut off the pride of the Philistines. And I will take away his blood out of his mouth, and his abominations from between his teeth: but he that remaineth, even he, shall be for our God, and he shall be as a governor in Judah, and Ekron as a Jebusite. And I will encamp about mine house because of the army, because of him that passeth by, and because of him that returneth: and no oppressor shall pass through them any more: for now have I seen with mine eyes. (Zechariah 9:1-8)

The Conquering of Alexander the Great (1-8): This chapter begins the "burden of the word of the LORD..." (1); a burden covering chapters 9-11. These verses deal with cutting off the pride of the Philistines (6). The instrument used to bring about the destruction of these cities is Alexander the Great. The Grecian armies led by Alexander are the belly and thighs of brass seen in the image of Nebuchadnezzar's dream (Daniel 2 cf. Zech. 9:13). Of all the cities conquered by Alexander probably none is more prophetically and historically documented as the destruction of Tyrus (3-4). The destruction of the city of Tyrus is prophesied in the book of Ezekiel, chapters 26-28. The following except is from *Ezekiel – The Glory of the LORD Has Departed*[9]:

"*Tyrus is mentioned in detail in chapters 26-28. The city is also mentioned in Isaiah 23 and*

---

[9] By this author

Jeremiah 27, however it is Ezekiel that Tyre is dealt with exclusively. Tyre was the ancient Phoenician city located at the site of present day Lebanon.

Hyram was king during the reigns of David and Solomon. He was a devoted friend, and he helped them both prepare for, and subsequently build, the temple (2 Samuel 5; I Kings 5; I Chronicles 14:2; 2 Chronicles 2). After the days of David and Solomon however, Tyre drifted away from Israel, and it finally got so bad that the people of Tyre sold Jews as slaves to the Greeks and the Edomites (Joel 3; Amos 1).

Tyre was the capital of the great Phoenician nation which was famous for its seagoing traders, and as such was a major trading center along routes from north to south. Thus, throughout these passages in Ezekiel and others, Tyre will be known as the land of 'traffick' and of 'merchants' (see chapter 27)."

The prophecy regarding the destruction of Tyre is pointed to as one of the most conclusive proof texts for the veracity of scripture.

The Prophecy of the Destruction of Jerusalem (1-21): The prophecy in these verses is about Nebuchadnezzar's attack on Tyre. But it was more than that; the Lord has more in view here than just the 13-year siege of Nebuchadnezzar and the "many nations" his empire consisted of.

The prophetic details given regarding the destruction of Tyrus assures us of the veracity of scripture. The specific verses detailing the destruction are found in Ezekiel 26:

(vs. 3) Therefore thus saith the Lord GOD; Behold, I am against thee, O Tyrus, and will cause many nations to come up against thee, as the sea causeth his waves to come up.

(vs. 4) And they shall destroy the walls of Tyrus, and break down her towers: I will also scrape her dust from her, and make her like the top of a rock.

(vs. 7) For thus saith the Lord GOD; Behold, I will bring upon Tyrus Nebuchadrezzar king of Babylon, a king of kings, from the north, with horses, and with chariots, and with horsemen, and companies, and much people.

(vs. 12) And they shall make a spoil of thy riches, and make a prey of thy merchandise: and they shall break down thy walls, and destroy thy pleasant houses: and they shall lay thy stones and thy timber and thy dust in the midst of the water.

(vs. 14) And I will make thee like the top of a rock: thou shalt be a place to spread nets upon; thou shalt be built no more: for I the LORD have spoken it, saith the Lord GOD.

(vs. 21) I will make thee a terror, and thou shalt be

no more: though thou be sought for, yet shalt thou never be found again, saith the Lord GOD.

The historical account that fulfills all these descriptions is as follows: Nebuchadnezzar came and laid siege on the city of Tyrus; for 13 years he cast a mount against it. No one could go in and no one could go out by land. Nebuchadnezzar had Tyrus in a strangle hold as he battled against the city. However, unbeknownst to Nebuchadnezzar, the people of Tyrus had loaded their ships, taking their people and their belongings to an island a half-mile out to sea. On this island they established a new city while their old one was under siege. Finally, Nebuchadnezzar knocked down the walls and entered the city. He came into Tyrus with all the nations of the world, for his army was made up of all the nations he had conquered. When Nebuchadnezzar entered the city he discovered that everyone was gone, with the exception of a few people; they had reestablished themselves as the new city of Tyrus, a half-mile out to sea. There they existed for some 200 years until a conquering leader known as Alexander the Great came. It was Alexander that would fulfill the rest of Ezekiel's prophecy. Alexander, like Nebuchadnezzar, ruled the known world at his time. Concerned about the fleet of ships that Tyrus possessed, Alexander sought to destroy them. He knew that there was only one way to destroy the island of Tyrus, and that was to make a land bridge out to sea to conquer the city. Alexander proceeded to take all the stones, timbers and debris from the old city of Tyrus, and cast it into the water to form his land bridge. He even used the dust from the old city to make mortar for his causeway, scraping the land clean like the top of a rock. Using this land bridge Alexander conquered the city of Tyrus. In Werner Keller's book *The Bible as History*, he outlines Alexander's attack on the Phoenician city of Tyrus:

> *"This city well-fortified and protected by stout high walls was built on a small island which guarded the coastline. Alexander performed here a miracle of military ingenuity by building a 2,000 foot mole in the sea out to the island city. To safeguard the operations, mobile protective shields, so-called "tortoises" had to be employed. Despite this the construction of the causeway was greatly hindered by an incessant hail of missiles. Meantime his engineers were on shore building veritable monsters: "Helepoleis." These were mobile protective towers many stories high, which held the detachments of bowmen and light artillery. A drawbridge on the front of the towers enabled a surprise attack to be made on the enemy's walls. They were the highest siege towers ever used in the history of war. Each of them had twenty stories and the topmost*

platform towered at a height of over 160 feet far above the highest city walls.

When after seven months preparation these monsters, bristling with weapons, slowly and clumsily rolled towards Tyre, the fate of the maritime stronghold, which was considered impregnable, was sealed."

Tyrus would continue to be rebuilt until Muslims completely annihilated the city in 1290 AD, never to rise again. To this day the only thing that exists is a small fishing village where any time of the day one can see men drying their nets. As to the old city of Tyrus, nothing remains. Something was rebuilt at the same site, but it was no more the ancient city of Tyrus than it was the city of Seattle.

In recapping the fulfilled prophecies of the destruction of Tyrus:

- **(vs. 3) Therefore thus saith the Lord GOD; Behold, I am against thee, O Tyrus, and will cause <u>many nations to come up against thee</u>, as the sea causeth his waves to come up.**

   Not only was Nebuchadnezzar's army made up of these "many nations" but many nations had come up against Tyrus until it was completely destroyed in 1290 AD.

- **(vs. 4 & 12) And they shall destroy the walls of Tyrus, and break down her towers: <u>I will</u>**

also scrape her dust from her, and make her like the top of a rock.

And they shall make a spoil of thy riches, and make a prey of thy merchandise: and they shall break down thy walls, and destroy thy pleasant houses: and they shall lay thy stones and thy timber and thy dust in the midst of the water. For thus saith the Lord GOD; When I shall make thee a desolate city, like the cities that are not inhabited; when I shall bring up the deep upon thee, and great waters shall cover thee;

During his campaign through Asia, Alexander ordered the rubble of the old Tyrus, which had been destroyed more than 200 years before, to be cast into the sea. Nothing was left behind but barren rock. With this rubble he built a causeway to attack the "new city" of Tyrus (333 BC), which had been rebuilt on the island, thus enabling him to conquer it.

• (vs. 7) For thus saith the Lord GOD; Behold, I will bring upon Tyrus Nebuchadrezzar king of Babylon, a king of kings, from the north, with horses, and with chariots, and with horsemen, and companies, and much people.

Nebuchadnezzar destroyed the city after a 13-year siege (585-573 BC). It was rebuilt on an island half-mile from the coast.

• (vs. 14) And I will make thee like the top of a

rock: thou shalt be a place to spread nets upon; thou shalt be built no more: for I the LORD have spoken it, saith the Lord GOD.

During the crusades Tyrus was finally brought to the ground by the Muslims; the old city of Tyrus was never rebuilt (1290 AD). Today the only thing remaining is a small fishing village where you can still see fishermen drying their nets.

- **(vs. 21) I will make thee a terror, <u>and thou shalt be no more: though thou be sought for, yet shalt thou never be found again</u>, saith the Lord GOD.**

The destruction of Tyrus was so complete that almost no stone was found in its original place.

Amazing as this is, there is also a most interesting event recorded by Flavius Josephus concerning Alexander and his military campaign to conquer the known world, and how it is that Alexander and his armies did not take the city of Jerusalem:

In 332 B.C. Alexander besieged and defeated the coastal cities of Tyre and Gaza in his march toward Egypt. During this campaign he turned toward Jerusalem. Alexander had already demanded men and supplies from the Jews, who were under the rule of Alexander's mortal enemy, the Persian king Darius. The high priest hesitated, saying that while Darius lived they would honor their pledge.

Alexander was angry and began a move on the city.

Well aware of the danger, Jaddua asked the people to pray to God for His mercy and protection. Then, says Josephus, Jaddua had a dream as to how to entreat the Macedonian king. He and the other priests dressed in their priestly robes and, accompanied by others dressed in white garments, formed a procession that went out of the city to a carefully chosen place to meet the king.

Alexander then did the unexpected. Alone, he approached the high priest and members of the procession and greeted them.

When asked by one of his generals why he welcomed this group, Alexander replied: "I did not adore him, but that God who hath honored him with his high priesthood; for I saw this very person in a dream, in this very habit [garment], when I was at Dios in Macedonia, who, when I was considering with myself how I might obtain the dominion of Asia, exhorted me to make no delay, but boldly to pass over the sea thither, for that he would conduct my army, and would give me the dominion over the Persians; whence it is, that having seen no other in that habit, and now seeing this person in it, and remembering that vision, and the exhortation which I had in my dream, I believe that I bring this army under the divine conduct, and shall therewith conquer Darius, and destroy the power of the Persians, and that all things will succeed according to what is in my own mind" (Josephus, *Antiquities of the Jews*, Book 11, chap. 8, sec. 5; William Whiston translation, 1977).

Josephus goes on to record that Alexander then accompanied the priest into Jerusalem and the temple, where he "offered sacrifice to God, according to the high priest's direction, and magnificently treated both the high priest and the priests."

Alexander's visit was topped off by a briefing from the book of Daniel, which foretold the rise and conquests of Grecian Empire.

"And when the book of Daniel was shewed him, wherein Daniel declared that one of the Greeks should destroy the empire of the Persians, he supposed that himself was the person intended; and as he was then glad, he dismissed the multitude for the present ..." (ibid.)

This historical event recorded by Flavius Josephus is most valuable, for in Zechariah chapter nine a prophetic announcement is given concerning a coming King, riding upon an ass, having salvation (Zech. 9:9). This is a major prophetical event that is given in the book of Daniel: "And after threescore and two weeks shall Messiah be cut off, but not for himself..." (Dan. 9:26). This cutting off of the Messiah is to happen following the Grecian Empire, during the Greco-Roman Empire, the legs of Iron of Daniel's image (Dan. 2).

Rejoice greatly, O daughter of Zion; shout, O daughter of Jerusalem: behold, thy King cometh unto thee: he is just, and having salvation; lowly, and riding upon an ass, and upon a colt the foal of an ass. And I will cut off the chariot from Ephraim, and the horse from Jerusalem, and the battle bow shall be cut off: and he shall speak peace unto the heathen: and his dominion shall be from sea even to sea, and from the river even to the ends of the earth. As for thee also, by the blood of thy covenant I have sent forth thy prisoners out of the pit wherein is no water. (Zechariah 9:9-11)

The Coming King (9-11): Following the military might of Alexander, the Grecian Empire was divided between his four generals. This structure was adopted by the ensuing Roman Empire, making Herod a Tetrarch (Luke 3:1) in the fourfold Greco-

Roman Empire, and fulfilling the role as the next world empire according to the prophet Daniel[10] (Dan. 2; 8:21; 10:20; 11). Daniel's prophecy also dates the time in which Israel's Messiah would come and present Himself in the way predicted by Zechariah:

Rejoice greatly, O daughter of Zion; shout, O daughter of Jerusalem: behold, thy King cometh unto thee: he is just, and having salvation; lowly, and riding upon an ass, and upon a colt the foal of an ass. (Zechariah 9:9)

In Daniel chapter nine, Daniel is told that from the going forth of the commandment to restore and rebuild Jerusalem until the coming of the Messiah, the Prince, shall be "seven weeks and threescore and two weeks" or a total of 483 years[11]:

Know therefore and understand, that from the going forth of the commandment to restore and to build Jerusalem unto the Messiah the Prince shall be seven weeks, and threescore and two weeks: the street shall be built again, and the wall, even in troublous times. (Daniel 9:25)

It is at the end of this 483 years, according to the prophecy given to Daniel, that the Messiah, the

---

[10] See author's booklet entitled *The Book of Daniel: Study Helps*

[11] For a detailed explanation of the time schedule, see this author's booklet entitled *The Book of Daniel: Study Helps,* pg. 41-43.

Prince, shall be in the land. It is also at the end of the 483 years that the Messiah would be "cut off" not for Himself, but for the sins of the people:

And after threescore and two weeks shall Messiah be cut off, but not for himself.... (Daniel 9:26 cf. Isa. 53).

All this was fulfilled exactly as the Scriptures had predicted. Jesus Christ, the Messiah of Israel, came to present Himself as the King of Israel following the 483 years (Luke 19:28-40), just as Daniel and Zechariah had predicted.

However, the nation rejected their King and therefore, what is described in verses 10 & 11 awaits a future fulfillment. Israel's King will come again and save them from their enemies, and establish His Kingdom on the earth. At that time His dominion will be from sea to sea and from river even to the ends of the earth:

The word that Isaiah the son of Amoz saw concerning Judah and Jerusalem. And it shall come to pass in the last days, that the mountain of the LORD'S house shall be established in the top of the mountains, and shall be exalted above the hills; and all nations shall flow unto it. And many people shall go and say, Come ye, and let us go up to the mountain of the LORD, to the house of the God of Jacob; and he will teach us of his ways, and

we will walk in his paths: for out of Zion shall go forth the law, and the word of the LORD from Jerusalem. And he shall judge among the nations, and shall rebuke many people: <u>and they shall beat their swords into plowshares, and their spears into pruninghooks: nation shall not lift up sword against nation, neither shall they learn war any more.</u> O house of Jacob, come ye, and let us walk in the light of the LORD. (Isaiah 2:1-5)

By the blood of the covenant the LORD is able to redeem His people from the pit wherein is no water (11). What an interesting verse. Many commentators would interpret this verse as prophetically referring to the time when the King of the Jews comes and delivers the Jews from the captivity of the armies of the Antichrist, prior to establishing His Kingdom. However, I believe it is looking at the redeeming of the prisoners from Hell; when our LORD shed His blood, and by the blood of this covenant, He overcame Hell and Death and delivered those who were the lawful captives in that abode. Our LORD delivered captives (See Eph. 4:8, 9 cf. Heb. 2:14, 15 cf. cf. Rev. 1:18 cf. Matt. 27:52, 53); He redeemed them from Hell, the pit where there is no water (Job 17:16, 33:24-28; Psalms 30:3, 40:2; Luke 16:24 cf. John 19:28) by the blood of the covenant, or the victory of His work on the cross (Isa. 49:24-26, 50:1, 5-9).

Turn you to the strong hold, ye prisoners of hope: even to day do I declare that I will render double unto thee; When I have bent Judah for me, filled the bow with Ephraim, and raised up thy sons, O Zion, against thy sons, O Greece, and made thee as the sword of a mighty man. And the LORD shall be seen over them, and his arrow shall go forth as the lightning: and the Lord GOD shall blow the trumpet, and shall go with whirlwinds of the south. The LORD of hosts shall defend them; and they shall devour, and subdue with sling stones; and they shall drink, and make a noise as through wine; and they shall be filled like bowls, and as the corners of the altar. And the LORD their God shall save them in that day as the flock of his people: for they shall be as the stones of a crown, lifted up as an ensign upon his land. For how great is his goodness, and how great is his beauty! corn shall make the young men cheerful, and new wine the maids. (Zechariah 9:12-17)

Future Revolts Leading to a Future Deliverance: In this final section our LORD looks into the future, at the time of Zechariah but historical for us. It is the time of the revolt of the Maccabees (12-13). During the reign of Antiochus Epiphanes, a group of Jews led a revolt against the Greeks, due in part to forced idolatry imposed upon them. The Maccabean revolt lasted some seven years, a time which Hanukkah commemorates.

However, while these passages do seem to point to such a time historically, the echoes of a yet future deliverance is in view. "The LORD of hosts shall defend them" (15) is the prophetic announcement. In the future the LORD will deliver His people Israel from the armies of the Antichrist at the battle of Armageddon, utilizing the earth (Rev. 12:16, 11:19, 16:21, Josh. 10:11; see notes on pages 132-133).

Once this deliverance takes place, Israel will be placed in her rightful position as head of the nations, a kingdom of priests (Ex. 19:6); making them that royal diadem, the crown of the LORD (16-17 cf. Mal. 3:17; Isa. 62:3).

CHAPTER TEN
The Re-gathering of the LORD

Ask ye of the LORD rain in the time of the latter rain; so the LORD shall make bright clouds, and give them showers of rain, to every one grass in the field. For the idols have spoken vanity, and the diviners have seen a lie, and have told false dreams; they comfort in vain: therefore they went their way as a flock, they were troubled, because there was no shepherd. Mine anger was kindled against the shepherds, and I punished the goats: for the LORD of hosts hath visited his flock the house of Judah, and hath made them as his goodly horse in the battle. Out of him came forth the corner, out of him the nail, out of him the battle bow, out of him every oppressor together. (Zechariah 10:1-4)

The Rightful Shepherd (1-4): Throughout the prophets, and up to the time of the Gospels, the

LORD rebuked the leadership of the nation. They, as the shepherds over His flock, cared not for them; their lack of care for the sheep of God was as if there was no shepherd at all (2). They let the nations of the earth prey on them and lead them into idolatry (2). Therefore the LORD's anger was kindled against the shepherds, the leadership of Israel (3), and in a future day the LORD, the true Shepherd of Israel, will seek His flock among the nations in which they were scattered. He will bring them back into the land and He will care for them. This whole passage is prophetically looking at that coming day; the day in which the LORD of hosts will visit His flock (3), the house of Judah, and will make them not as His sheep but as His goodly horse in battle. (See all of Ezekiel 34, John 10:1-18 and chart on page 117 for insight and details concerning the LORD functioning as the Shepherd of Israel).

And they shall be as mighty men, which tread down their enemies in the mire of the streets in the battle: and they shall fight, because the LORD is with them, and the riders on horses shall be confounded. And I will strengthen the house of Judah, and I will save the house of Joseph, and I will bring them again to place them; for I have mercy upon them: and they shall be as though I had not cast them off: for I am the LORD their

God, and will hear them. And they of Ephraim shall be like a mighty man, and their heart shall rejoice as through wine: yea, their children shall see it, and be glad; their heart shall rejoice in the LORD. I will hiss for them, and gather them; for I have redeemed them: and they shall increase as they have increased. And I will sow them among the people: and they shall remember me in far countries; and they shall live with their children, and turn again. I will bring them again also out of the land of Egypt, and gather them out of Assyria; and I will bring them into the land of Gilead and Lebanon; and place shall not be found for them. And he shall pass through the sea with affliction, and shall smite the waves in the sea, and all the deeps of the river shall dry up: and the pride of Assyria shall be brought down, and the sceptre of Egypt shall depart away. And I will strengthen them in the LORD; and they shall walk up and down in his name, saith the LORD. (Zechariah 10:5-12)

The Gathering of the God's People (5-12): The future re-gathering and deliverance of the Jewish people is the subject of the remaining verses in this chapter. This chapter, and those following, all tie together regarding the shepherds of Israel. We begin with the shepherds over Israel that the LORD rejected (Zech. 10:1-4), and we see the Lord Jesus Christ, the true Shepherd over Israel who came to seek those sheep that were lost (John 10:11-17). The apostate shepherds however rejected the true Shepherd (Zech. 11:12-13; 13:7). This rejection of their true Shepherd leads to the nation receiving the idol shepherd, who will not care for the sheep of Israel but devour them (Zech. 11:15-17). Under the persecution of the idol shepherd, the nation will cry out to God, and the true Shepherd of Israel will come to deliver His sheep, to re-gather and place them in His pasture (Zech. 13:8-9; Ezek. 34:11-19). It is this re-gathering from among the nations that Zechariah is speaking of in these verses, and others to follow. Historically, at the time of Zechariah, a remnant is being re-gathered from Babylonian captivity, which makes it perfectly fitting for the LORD to record by the mouth of Zechariah a prophetical re-gathering coming for His people:

And I will strengthen the house of Judah, and <u>I will save the house of Joseph, and I will bring them again to place them; for I have mercy upon them: and they shall be as though I had not cast them off</u>: for I am the LORD their God, and will hear them. And they of Ephraim shall be like a mighty man, and their heart shall rejoice as through wine: yea, their children shall see it, and be glad; their heart shall rejoice in the LORD. <u>I will hiss for them, and gather them; for I have redeemed them: and they shall increase as they have increased.</u> And I will sow them among the

110

people: and they shall remember me in far countries; and they shall live with their children, and turn again. <u>I will bring them again also out of the land of Egypt, and gather them out of Assyria; and I will bring them into the land of Gilead and Lebanon;</u> and place shall not be found for them. (Zechariah 10:6-10)

CHAPTER ELEVEN
The Idol Shepherd

Open thy doors, O Lebanon, that the fire may devour thy cedars. Howl, fir tree; for the cedar is fallen; because the mighty are spoiled: howl, O ye oaks of Bashan; for the forest of the vintage is come down. There is a voice of the howling of the shepherds; for their glory is spoiled: a voice of the roaring of young lions; for the pride of Jordan is spoiled. Thus saith the LORD my God; Feed the flock of the slaughter; Whose possessors slay them, and hold themselves not guilty: and they that sell them say, Blessed be the LORD; for I am rich: and their own shepherds pity them not. For I will no more pity the inhabitants of the land, saith the LORD: but, lo, I will deliver the men every one into his neighbour's hand, and into the hand of his king: and they shall smite the land, and out of their hand I will not deliver them. And I will feed the flock of slaughter, even you, O poor of the flock. And I took unto me two staves; the one I called Beauty, and the other I called Bands; and I fed the flock. Three shepherds also I cut off in one month; and my soul lothed them, and their soul also abhorred me. Then said I, I will not feed you: that that dieth, let it die; and that that is to be cut off, let it be cut off; and let the rest eat every one the flesh of another. (Zechariah 11:1-9)

The Suffering of the People at the Hands of the Shepherds (1-9): Because the shepherds, the leadership (both kings and religious leaders), ruling Israel would not harken unto the voice of their true Shepherd, the people suffered. The leadership over Israel harkened to false prophets and the unwise council of the priests, rather than the LORD. Thus, the judgments of the LORD against Israel's leadership (the shepherds) fell on the people of God:

For the leaders of this people cause them to err; and they that are led of them are destroyed. (Isaiah 9:16)

For I will no more pity the inhabitants of the land, saith the LORD: but, lo, I will deliver the men every one into his neighbour's hand, and into the hand of his king: and they shall smite the land, and out of their hand I will not deliver them. (Zechariah 11:6)

The rebuke in these verses is once again against the shepherds, the leadership over the people; notice the following:

- Their glory (the shepherds) is spoiled (vs. 3)

- Whose possessors (the shepherds) slay them (the people), and hold themselves not guilty (vs. 5)
- They that sell them (the leadership is selling the people to destruction) say, blessed be the LORD; for I am rich (vs. 5)
- Their own shepherds pity them not (vs. 5)

It was the shepherds of Israel that had led the nation astray. The shepherds were to feed the flock of Israel (i.e. care for them), but instead they only cared for themselves (Ezek. 34:2-3). By the time of the Gospels, when the true Shepherd over Israel was in the land, not much had changed (John 10).

And I took my staff, even Beauty, and cut it asunder, that I might break my covenant which I had made with all the people. And it was broken in that day: and so the poor of the flock that waited upon me knew that it was the word of the LORD. And I said unto them, If ye think good, give me my price; and if not, forbear. So they weighed for my price thirty pieces of silver. And the LORD said unto me, Cast it unto the potter: a goodly price that I was prised at of them. And I took the thirty pieces of silver, and cast them to the potter in the house of the LORD. Then I cut asunder mine other

staff, even Bands, that I might break the brotherhood between Judah and Israel. (Zechariah 11:10-14)

The Two Broken Staffs of the LORD (10-14): This section really begins in verse 7 with the two staffs: *And I will feed the flock of slaughter, even you, O poor of the flock. And I took unto me two staves; the one I called Beauty, and the other I called Bands; and I fed the flock. (Zechariah 11:7)*

A staff is something that is leaned on or trusted in (see negatively since 2 Kings 18:21). The nation of Israel trusted in their covenant made with the LORD, the staff of Beauty (vs. 10) and they trusted in their strength as the twelve tribes (vs. 14 cf. Lev. 26:19 cf. I Kings 12-22). By the context it would seem that the covenant between the nation and the LORD was broken at the betrayal of Jesus Christ (11-13 cf. Matt. 26:15; 27:9). The leadership of the nation, through Judas Iscariot, rejected Jesus Christ for thirty pieces of silver. It is this rejection of the true Shepherd that leads to the nation receiving the false, or idol, shepherd (15-17).

And the LORD said unto me, Take unto thee yet the instruments of a foolish shepherd. For, lo, I will raise up a shepherd in the land, which shall not visit those that be cut off, neither shall seek the young one, nor heal that that is broken, nor feed that that standeth still: but he shall eat the flesh of the fat, and tear their claws in pieces. Woe to the idol shepherd that leaveth the flock! the sword shall be upon his arm, and upon his right eye: his arm shall be clean dried up, and his right eye shall be utterly darkened. (Zechariah 11:15-17)

The Idol Shepherd (15-17): Chapters 10-12 flow in unison regarding the shepherds of Israel. In chapter ten the LORD condemns the shepherds that disobeyed the LORD and led their people (the flock) astray (10:1-4). Then in this chapter they reject the true Shepherd that came to seek out the flock of Israel, and deliver them from the apostate leadership (11:10-13); they will therefore receive the foolish or idol shepherd, the Antichrist (11:15-17). Lastly, in chapter 12 the people of God will cry out to their rejected Shepherd because of the great persecution they will be suffering under the idol shepherd (12:10 cf. chapter 13), and He will deliver them (chapters 13:8-9 cf. 14).

OLD TESTAMENT	GOSPELS		TRIBULATION		MILLENNIUM
Rebuke of the wicked shepherds (Ezek. 34:1-10)	True Shepherd comes (John 10)	True Shepherd rejected (Zech. 11:12,13)	Idol shepherd received (Zech. 11:15-17)	Flock cries out to the True Shepherd (Zech. 12:9, 10)	True Shepherd delivers His flock and brings them into the pasture (Ezek. 34:11-19)

✝

A description of the Antichrist is given in these verses. Because of the leadership's rejection of the true Shepherd, the LORD will raise up a foolish shepherd that will do the exact opposite of what a shepherd is supposed to do, take care of the flock:

- The idol shepherd does not visit those that are cut off (16)
- The idol shepherd seeks not the young ones (16)
- The idol shepherd does not heal the broken (16)
- The idol shepherd feeds not the flock (16)
- The idol shepherd will devour the flock (16)
- The idol shepherd leaves the flock (17)

The exact opposite was true when our LORD came in His first advent, as the true Shepherd over Israel:

- The true Shepherd came to seek the lost of the flock (Luke 15:1-4 cf. Matt. 15:24)
- The true Shepherd healed the broken of His flock (Matt. 10:5-8)
- The true Shepherd came to feed the flock (John 21:15-17)
- The true Shepherd protected them from the wolves (Matt. 7:15; 10:16)
- The true Shepherd will never leave His flock (Matt. 28:20)

The last verse is a physical description of the Antichrist, the idol shepherd that is to come (17). It would seem that his "dried up right arm" and his "darkened right eye" are the result of this military general surviving a deadly wound (Rev. 13:12). This could also be the reason he will demand his mark be put on the forehead or hand of all who are to buy and sell (Rev. 14:9). The following is some biblical information concerning this coming world leader, known in this passage as the foolish or idol shepherd:

- He will be a military leader, controlling a great army and able to bring peace to the Middle East (Psalms 83)
- He will survive a deadly wound that will leave his right hand dried up and his right eye darkened *(Rev. 13:12 cf. Zech. 11:17)*
- He will be a wonder to all the nations, preforming signs and miracles *(Rev. 17:8 cf. 2 Thess. 2:9)*
- He will control the world's economy *(Rev. 13:17)*
- He will cause the world to worship his image and receive his mark *(Rev. 13:12-15)*
- He will lead the nations against Israel in an effort to abolish them *(Psalms 83 cf. Daniel 11:40)*
- He will desecrate the Temple of the LORD, claiming to be God *(2 Thess. 2:4)*

- He will lead a final army against the armies of the LORD *(Rev. 19:19)*

- He will be cast alive into the lake of fire *(Rev. 19:19-20 cf. 20:10)*

CHAPTER TWELVE
Deliverance of the Flock of God

The burden of the word of the LORD for Israel, saith the LORD, which stretcheth forth the heavens, and layeth the foundation of the earth, and formeth the spirit of man within him. Behold, I will make Jerusalem a cup of trembling unto all the people round about, when they shall be in the siege both against Judah and against Jerusalem. (Zechariah 12:1-2)

A Cup of Trembling unto all People (1-2): This whole chapter deals with the deliverance of the flock of God by the true Shepherd, the LORD Jesus Christ. The time of this deliverance is the end of the Tribulation Period when the LORD returns. It is designated by the phrase "in that day" throughout this chapter, and is defined in Ezekiel: *For thus saith the Lord GOD; Behold, I, even I, will both search my sheep, and seek them out. As a shepherd seeketh out his* *flock in the day that he is among his sheep that are scattered; so will I seek out my sheep, and will deliver them out of all places where they have been scattered in the cloudy and dark day. (Ezekiel 34:11-12)*

The "dark and cloudy day" is none other than the end of the Tribulation period (Amos 5:20 cf. Isa. 60:1-3). Specifically, it will be when all nations gather themselves together against the people of God at Jerusalem, a time known as the battle of Armageddon (Rev. 19:19 cf. 16:16 cf. Zeph. 3:8 Zech. 9:9, 12:3).

And in that day will I make Jerusalem a burdensome stone for all people: all that burden themselves with it shall be cut in pieces, though all the people of the earth be gathered together against it. In that day, saith the LORD, I will smite every horse with astonishment, and his rider with madness: and I will open mine eyes upon the house of Judah, and will smite every horse of the people with blindness. And the governors of Judah shall say in their heart, The inhabitants of Jerusalem shall be my strength in the LORD of hosts their God. In that day will I make the governors of Judah like an hearth of fire among the wood, and like a torch of fire in a sheaf; and they shall devour all the people round about, on the right hand and on the left: and Jerusalem shall

be inhabited again in her own place, even in Jerusalem. The LORD also shall save the tents of Judah first, that the glory of the house of David and the glory of the inhabitants of Jerusalem do not magnify themselves against Judah. In that day shall the LORD defend the inhabitants of Jerusalem; and he that is feeble among them at that day shall be as David; and the house of David shall be as God, as the angel of the LORD before them. (Zechariah 12:3-8)

Jerusalem, the Burdensome Stone (3-8): All that try and come against Jerusalem will be "cut in pieces," for the LORD will defend and deliver His flock. The LORD's return is in view throughout these verses and this chapter, and is vividly depicted in Revelation 19 and Isaiah 63. The LORD promises to "defend the inhabitants of Jerusalem" (8). This event will precede the remnant of Israel receiving their Messiah whom they crucified (vs10 cf. 13:6); once they call out to Him, He will come and deliver His people and establish the New Covenant with them (see Ezekiel 36).

And it shall come to pass in that day, that I will seek to destroy all the nations that come against Jerusalem. And I will pour upon the house of David, and upon the inhabitants of Jerusalem, the spirit of grace and of supplications: and they shall look upon me whom they have pierced, and they shall mourn for him, as one mourneth for his only son, and shall be in bitterness for him, as one that is in bitterness for his firstborn. In that day shall there be a great mourning in Jerusalem, as the mourning of Hadadrimmon in the valley of Megiddon. And the land shall mourn, every family apart; the family of the house of David apart, and their wives apart; the family of the house of Nathan apart, and their wives apart; The family of the house of Levi apart, and their wives apart; the family of Shimei apart, and their wives apart; All the families that remain, every family apart, and their wives apart. (Zechariah 12:9-14)

Receiving the Pierced Messiah (9-14): The Remnant of Israel will one day receive their crucified Messiah, the one whom they have pierced (10). This will all be part of the conversion of the Remnant that will mark the LORD coming to the earth to deliver Israel. The conversion of the Remnant of Israel is the subject of these verses, especially verse 10. Just as Peter preached the need of repentance for killing their Messiah to the believing Jews in the book of Acts:

Men and brethren, let me freely speak unto you of the patriarch David, that he is both dead and buried, and his sepulchre is with us unto this day. Therefore being a prophet, and knowing that God had sworn with an oath to him, that of the fruit of his loins, according to the flesh, he would raise up Christ to sit on his throne; He seeing this before spake of the resurrection of Christ, that his soul was not left in hell, neither his flesh did see corruption. This Jesus hath God raised up, whereof we all are witnesses. Therefore being by the right hand of God exalted, and having received of the Father the promise of the Holy Ghost, he hath shed forth this, which ye now see and hear. For David is not ascended into the heavens: but he saith himself, The LORD said unto my Lord, Sit thou on my right hand, Until I make thy foes thy footstool. Therefore let all the house of Israel know assuredly, that God hath made that same Jesus, whom ye have crucified, both Lord and Christ. Now when they heard this, they were pricked in their heart, and said unto Peter and to the rest of the apostles, Men and brethren, what shall we do? Then Peter said unto them, Repent, and be baptized every one of you in the name of Jesus Christ for the remission of sins, and ye shall receive the gift of the Holy Ghost. For the promise is unto you, and to your children, and to all that are afar off, even as many as the Lord our God shall call. And with many other words did he testify and exhort, saying, Save yourselves from this untoward generation. (Acts 2:29-40)

And when Peter saw it, he answered unto the people, Ye men of Israel, why marvel ye at this? or why look ye so earnestly on us, as though by our own power or holiness we had made this man to walk? The God of Abraham, and of Isaac, and of Jacob, the God of our fathers, hath glorified his Son Jesus; whom ye delivered up, and denied him in the presence of Pilate, when he was determined to let him go. But ye denied the Holy One and the Just, and desired a murderer to be granted unto you; And killed the Prince of life, whom God hath raised from the dead; whereof we are witnesses. And his name through faith in his name hath made this man strong, whom ye see and know: yea, the faith which is by him hath given him this perfect soundness in the presence of you all. And now, brethren, I wot that through ignorance ye did it, as did also your rulers. But those things, which God before had shewed by the mouth of all his prophets, that Christ should suffer, he hath so fulfilled. Repent ye therefore, and be converted, that your sins may be blotted out, when the times of refreshing shall come from the presence of the Lord; And he shall send Jesus Christ, which before was preached unto you: (Acts 3:12-20)

At the time Peter preached this message a Remnant did believe, but the nation as a whole refused to "repent" and went even further in their rebellion of rejecting the Holy Ghost by the stoning of Stephen (Acts 7). Thus, the LORD Jesus Christ did not come back, nor did the times of refreshing come. All this therefore awaits a future day in which the nation will look on Him whom they have pierced and mourn for Him as one mourns for his only son; at that time He will pour out His Spirit and they shall be converted. It is then that the times of refreshing shall be established, and the sins of the entire nation shall be forgiven:

And I will pour upon the house of David, and upon the inhabitants of Jerusalem, the spirit of grace and of supplications: and they shall look upon me whom they have pierced, and they shall mourn for him, as one mourneth for his only son, and shall be in bitterness for him, as one that is in bitterness for his firstborn. (Zechariah 12:10) – see also Isaiah 66:8; Joel 2; Ezekiel 37.

The great mourning will be likened to the time when the nation of Judah mourned over King Josiah upon his death (vs. cf. 2 Kings 23:29-30 cf. 2 Chron. 35:22-27). The word "apart," repeated in verses 12 & 13 in relation to mourning, is significant to the idea of mourning alone, turning away to mourn in private with great lamenting. All this is to illustrate the great repentance of the future Remnant of the Jews over the reality that they crucified the LORD's Anointed.

CHAPTER THIRTEEN
Purging of the Land

In that day there shall be a fountain opened to the house of David and to the inhabitants of Jerusalem for sin and for uncleanness. (Zechariah 13:1)

A Fountain for Cleansing (1): This chapter is following the previous chapter dealing with the conversion of Israel, the LORD's deliverance of them and their cleansing and establishment. The fountain that is opened to the house of David is a literal fountain flowing from the future Millennial Temple (Ezekiel 47:1-12 cf. Zech. 14:8-9 cf. Revelation 22:1-2).

And it shall come to pass in that day, saith the LORD of hosts, that I will cut off the names of the idols out of the land, and they shall no more be remembered: and also I will cause the prophets and the unclean spirit to pass out of the land. And it shall come to pass, that when any shall yet

prophesy, then his father and his mother that begat him shall say unto him, Thou shalt not live; for thou speakest lies in the name of the LORD: and his father and his mother that begat him shall thrust him through when he prophesieth. And it shall come to pass in that day, that the prophets shall be ashamed every one of his vision, when he hath prophesied; neither shall they wear a rough garment to deceive: But he shall say, I am no prophet, I am an husbandman; for man taught me to keep cattle from my youth. And one shall say unto him, What are these wounds in thine hands? Then he shall answer, Those with which I was wounded in the house of my friends. (Zechariah 13:2-6)

Purging of the Kingdom (2-6): Once the LORD returns He will deliver His people from the armies of the antichrist and then He will begin to purge the land of all ungodly elements and its filthiness in the land (see Matt. 13:41). Thus, the idols, prophets and unclean spirits shall pass out of the land (vs. 2). The LORD will be sitting on the throne of His glory ruling as King and therefore the need for prophets during this time will be done away. As Isaiah tells us if they need to know a word from the LORD all they need to do is simply go up to the house of the LORD and ask Him:

And it shall come to pass in the last days, that the mountain of the LORD'S house shall be established in the top of the mountains, and shall be exalted above the hills; and all nations shall flow unto it. And many people shall go and say, Come ye, and let us go up to the mountain of the LORD, to the house of the God of Jacob; and he will teach us of his ways, and we will walk in his paths: for out of Zion shall go forth the law, and the word of the LORD from Jerusalem. (Isaiah 2:2-3)

In this passage the prophet that prophesy will be punished by his own family (vs. 3) receiving wounds in the house of his friends (vs. 6). This passage echo's out to the Prophet who came and was wounded in the house of His friends (Mark 3:21 cf. John 1:11), the LORD Jesus Christ. Therefore the next verse deal with the rejection of the God Man, Jesus Christ, the True Shepherd of Israel.

Awake, O sword, against my shepherd, and against the man that is my fellow, saith the LORD of hosts: smite the shepherd, and the sheep shall be scattered: and I will turn mine hand upon the little ones. And it shall come to pass, that in all the land, saith the LORD, two parts therein shall be cut off and die; but the third shall be left therein. And I will bring the third part through the fire, and will refine them as silver is refined, and will try them as gold is tried: they shall call on my name, and I

will hear them: I will say, It is my people: and they shall say, The LORD is my God. (Zechariah 13:7-9)

Salvation of the Remnant of Israel (7-9): This portion of scripture is highly prophetic looking out to the time during the Tribulation Period in which the LORD bring the Remnant of His people through that most horrific time.

While the LORD was on earth He prepared His little flock for the coming Kingdom (Luke 12:32). The LORD knowing of His coming rejection by His own people prepared a Remnant of believing Israelites, His Apostles to function in His absence. Upon the LORD's crucifixion the bulk of Israel would be scattered in unbelief (vs. 7); however, it would be at this time that a believing Remnant would be formed and would carry on the preaching of the gospel of the Kingdom until the LORD returned to establish that very Kingdom. This very thing began to unfold in the Gospels and Acts period, however was put on hold for the ushering in of the Dispensation of the Grace of God, proclaimed by the Apostle Paul. The nation will once again be scattered by the armies of the antichrist, it will be at this time however that the LORD will once again "turn His hand upon the little ones", His Remnant. It will be at this time that they will "look on Him whom they have pierced and mourn for them as one mourns for his only son" (vs. 12:10). The LORD will then pour out His Spirit, they will be converted and enabled to preach the Gospel of the Kingdom and brought through the fire of God's wrath (Tribulation Period) into His Kingdom. Thus, this Remnant is the "third part that will be brought through the fire" and then the last part of verse nine will be fulfilled:

And I will bring the third part through the fire, and will refine them as silver is refined, and will try them as gold is tried: they shall call on my name, and I will hear them: I will say, It is my people: and they shall say, The LORD is my God. (vs. 9 cf. I Peter 1:7)[12]

---

[12] The Type of this Remnant going through the wrath of the LORD upon His return is found in Daniel chapter 3 and the three Hebrews that are cast into the fiery furnace and live by the help of the LORD Jesus Christ (see Dan. 3:25).

CHAPTER FOURTEEN
The Return of the LORD &
the Establishment of the
Theocratic Kingdom

Behold, the day of the LORD cometh, and thy spoil shall be divided in the midst of thee. For I will gather all nations against Jerusalem to battle; and the city shall be taken, and the houses rifled, and the women ravished; and half of the city shall go forth into captivity, and the residue of the people shall not be cut off from the city. Then shall the LORD go forth, and fight against those nations, as when he fought in the day of battle. (Zechariah 14:1-3)

The Avenging of the LORD (1-3): This last chapter covers events surrounding the return of the LORD and the establishment of the Kingdom. At some point in the final days prior to the LORD's return all nations will come against Israel to seek to obliterate it and it's people. The nations mentioned here are those Arab nations that surround the nation of Israel, the very ones that have always been the enemies of God's people. The nations will seek a covenant of peace with Israel, however their real intentions are to annihilate the people in the hopes that the name of Israel be no more mentioned on the face of the earth. Psalm 83 gives us great insight into this false covenant of peace:

For, lo, thine enemies make a tumult: and they that hate thee have lifted up the head. They have taken crafty counsel against thy people, and consulted against thy hidden ones. They have said, Come, and let us cut them off from being a nation; that the name of Israel may be no more in remembrance. For they have consulted together with one consent: they are confederate against thee: (Psalms 83:2-5)

This event is named the Battle of Armageddon (Rev. 16:16) and it will be at this event that the LORD comes back and fights for Israel (vs. 3). When the LORD comes back into the land He will come a certain route fighting wars as He comes up into Jerusalem to deliver Israel (Isaiah 63). He will fight against those nations that are confederate against God's people (Psalm 83 cf. Joel 3:9-16) as when He fought in the day of Battle. This "day of battle" is a reference to the time which the LORD miraculously fought for Israel as they were conquering the Promised Land:

And the LORD said unto Joshua, Fear them not: for I have delivered them into thine hand; there shall not a man of them stand before thee. Joshua therefore came unto them suddenly, and went up from Gilgal all night. And

134

the LORD discomfited them before Israel, and slew them with a great slaughter at Gibeon, and chased them along the way that goeth up to Bethhoron, and smote them to Azekah, and unto Makkedah. And it came to pass, as they fled from before Israel, and were in the going down to Bethhoron, that the LORD cast down great stones from heaven upon them unto Azekah, and they died: they were more which died with hailstones than they whom the children of Israel slew with the sword. (Joshua 10:8-11)

The LORD fought with great hailstones that day and did other miraculous events such as stopping the sun and the moon (10:12-14). So then upon the LORD's future return to deliver Israel and establish His Kingdom the LORD will use His creation to judge the earth and those nations that come against His people, it will be as when He fought in the day of battle:

Hast thou entered into the treasures of the snow? or hast thou seen the treasures of the hail, Which I have reserved against the time of trouble, against the day of battle and war? (Job 38:22-23)

And he gathered them together into a place called in the Hebrew tongue Armageddon. (Revelation 16:16)

And there fell upon men a great hail out of heaven, every stone about the weight of a talent: and men blasphemed God because of the plague of the hail; for the plague thereof was exceeding great. (Revelation 16:21)

And his feet shall stand in that day upon the mount of Olives, which is before Jerusalem on the east, and the mount of Olives shall cleave in the midst thereof toward the east and toward the west, and there shall be a very great valley; and half of the mountain shall remove toward the north, and half of it toward the south. And ye shall flee to the valley of the mountains; for the valley of the mountains shall reach unto Azal: yea, ye shall flee, like as ye fled from before the earthquake in the days of Uzziah king of Judah: and the LORD my God shall come, and all the saints with thee. (Zechariah 14:4-5)

The Return of the King (4-5): The great subject of the prophets look forward to the time when the LORD will establish His Kingdom on the earth (vs. 9). It is how, when, where and why of this great subject that is foretold in the scriptures. In verses 4 through 5 you have the return of the LORD to Jerusalem and in verses 6 thorough 11 you have details concerning the Kingdoms establishment. When the LORD returns He will return into Jerusalem in the way in which He departed. According to Ezekiel, the Glory of the LORD departed through the eastern gate across the Kidron Valley to the Mount of Olives (Ezekiel 11:23); and when our LORD ascended back to glory after appearing to His disciples upon His resurrection He departed from the Mount of Olives (Acts 1:9-12).

Thus, Zechariah sees the LORD's feet touching the Mount of Olives upon His Second Advent and in so doing He splits the Mount of Olives in two creating a valley running from the Eastern Gate, east to west (4). The purpose of this valley created by the descending of our LORD would seem to be twofold:

- The Kidron Valley which is also the Valley of Jehoshaphat is directly between the Mount of Olives and the Eastern Gate. It is this valley that the armies of the antichrist will come up to destroy Israel (Joel 3:2-16). Therefore the valley created by the splitting of the Mount of Olives would directly intersects the Kidron Valley making way to the Eastern Gate and a route for not only the deliverance of God's people (vs. 5) but also a path to utterly destroy those nations come to seek the destruction of Israel.

- Once the Millennial Temple is established there will be a river that will flow out the Eastern Gate where it will flow in two directions one branch towards the Dead Sea and the other towards the Mediterranean Sea (Ezekiel 47:1-12 cf. Zech. 14:8). The cleaving of the Mount of Olives could make the way for this river.

Those who flee at the return of the LORD to the Mount of Olives and the splitting of that mountain is likened to the time of the great earthquake during the reign of Uzziah King of Judah (5 cf. Amos 1:1). Josephus ties this earthquake to the time in which Uzziah attempted to offer incense in the temple against the protests of the priests (2 Chron. 26; 16:21).[13]

The LORD will come with His armies, "the LORD my God shall come and all the saints with thee." Saints in the Bible is used for angels (Deut. 33:3; Job 15:15) and of holy men (Psalm 16:3, 34:9, 50:5; Lev. 11:44, 45) of redeemed Israel (Daniel 7:21-22 cf. Matt. 27:52; Rev. 14:12; 20:9) and redeemed people (Acts 9:13, 32, 41; Romans 1:7, 12:13, 15:25; I Cor. 1:2; 2 Cor. 1:1).

And it shall come to pass in that day, that the light shall not be clear, nor dark: But it shall be one day which shall be known to the LORD, not day, nor night: but it shall come to pass, that at evening time it shall be light. And it shall be in that day, that living waters shall go out from Jerusalem; half of them toward the former sea, and half of them toward the hinder sea: in summer and in winter shall it be. And the LORD shall be king over all the earth: in that day shall there be one LORD, and his name one. All the land shall be turned as a plain from Geba to Rimmon south of Jerusalem:

---

[13] Antiquities IX, 10, 4.

and it shall be lifted up, and inhabited in her place, from Benjamin's gate unto the place of the first gate, unto the corner gate, and from the tower of Hananeel unto the king's winepresses. And men shall dwell in it, and there shall be no more utter destruction; but Jerusalem shall be safely inhabited. (Zechariah 14:6-11)

The Landscape of the Kingdom to Come (6-11): Once the LORD comes and delivers Israel the LORD will establish Himself as Monarch on the earth (vs. 9). In His establishing of His Kingdom many changes to the region will transpire, not only listed here in theses verse but throughout the prophets and the book of Revelation. Once the LORD's Kingdom is established Zechariah notes the following changes:

- Within the Kingdom there will be no need for the sun, for there will be light emanating from the throne that will lighten the Kingdom (vs. 6-7 cf. Rev. 21:23)
- Waters will come forth from the throne in the Millennial Temple, heading out easten direction; it will then branch off to flow to the Mediterranean Sea and the Dead Sea, which it will revive (vs. 8 cf. Joel 3:18, Rev. 22:1-2; Ezek. 47:1-2).
- All the land described in verse 10 will be as a plain. Notice it is very literal, exact locations are given.

- Their shall be no more utter destruction, it will be a Kingdom of Peace (vs. 11 cf. Isa. 2:4; Mic. 4:3).

And this shall be the plague wherewith the LORD will smite all the people that have fought against Jerusalem; Their flesh shall consume away while they stand upon their feet, and their eyes shall consume away in their holes, and their tongue shall consume away in their mouth. And it shall come to pass in that day, that a great tumult from the LORD shall be among them; and they shall lay hold every one on the hand of his neighbour, and his hand shall rise up against the hand of his neighbour. And Judah also shall fight at Jerusalem; and the wealth of all the heathen round about shall be gathered together, gold, and silver, and apparel, in great abundance. And so shall be the plague of the horse, of the mule, of the camel, and of the ass, and of all the beasts that shall be in these tents, as this plague. (Zechariah 14:12-15)

The Plague of the LORD (12-15): Before the LORD comes and establishes His Kingdom, He will vanquish Israel's enemies under the leadership of the antichrist. The LORD will cause a plague to go forth that will literally consume their bodies while they stand on their feet (12). This plague will cause the armies of the antichrist to begin to fight one another, much like what happened during the days of Jehoshaphat (vs. 13 cf. 2 Chron. 20:22-24). This plague will consume even the livestock (15). The Jewish people will receive power of the LORD to help in the fight at the LORD's return (vs. 14 cf. 12:8) and once victory is accomplished they will receive the spoils of war (14).

And it shall come to pass, that every one that is left of all the nations which came against Jerusalem shall even go up from year to year to worship the King, the LORD of hosts, and to keep the feast of tabernacles. And it shall be, that whoso will not come up of all the families of the earth unto Jerusalem to worship the King, the LORD of hosts, even upon them shall be no rain. And if the family of Egypt go not up, and come not, that have no rain; there shall be the plague, wherewith the LORD will smite the heathen that come not up to keep the feast of tabernacles. This shall be the punishment of Egypt, and the punishment of all nations that come not up to keep the feast of tabernacles. (Zechariah 14:16-19)

The Feast of Tabernacles (16-19): Upon the establishment of the LORD's Kingdom the people of the Kingdom will institute the Feast of Tabernacles to all the nations that survived the battle of the LORD (16). Those nations will also be called upon to worship the King, the LORD of hosts coming up to Jerusalem form year to year (16). This feast was celebrated when the Jewish people returned from exile (Neh. 8:14-18). All the nations and families of the earth that refuse to come up to worship the King and observe the Feast of Tabernacles at Jerusalem from year to year shall befall the plague of drought, no rain (17-19).[14]

In that day shall there be upon the bells of the horses, HOLINESS UNTO THE LORD; and the pots in the LORD'S house shall be like the bowls before the altar. Yea, every pot in Jerusalem and in Judah shall be holiness unto the LORD of hosts: and all they that sacrifice shall come and take of them, and seethe therein: and in that day there shall be no more the Canaanite in the house of the LORD of hosts. (Zechariah 14:20-21)

Holiness Unto the LORD (20-21): This book finishes with a glimpse into the Glory of the coming Kingdom. One of the main characteristics of the future Kingdom will be "HOLINESS UNTO THE LORD" (Isa. 35:8; Joel 3:17).

---

[14] It would seem that this drought of rain would be for a calendar year until the opportunity to attend the Feast of Tabernacles would come around.

Conclusion

Zechariah means "The Lord remembers", it is this title that encompasses the thought behind the book as a whole. The LORD has not forgotten all the promises He has made to His people. At the time of Zechariah things were looking bright, they have just come out of 70 years of servitude in the Babylonian empire and they are building the temple and reinstituting Levitical worship. However, they are still struggling to gain any independence from the Gentile kingdoms. The picture at the time of Zechariah of the Jewish people is far from what the LORD has promised in the scriptures by the mouth of the prophets. Is there still hope for their future as God's chosen people? Will our LORD come and deliver them from this Gentile oppression? Or has their willful disobedience caused the LORD to turn His back on His people?

The book of Zechariah answers these questions with "the Lord remembers." On every page of Zechariah the Lord shows through prophetic passages that He has not forgotten His people or the promises He has made to them. In vivid detail he tells of His future return to deliver the Jewish people from the Gentile nations and the future establishment of His long-awaited kingdom. He is their hope and through the prophet Zechariah (and Haggai) they are continually reminded that the LORD does remember.

THE BOOK OF HAGGAI

Consider Your Ways

Introduction

The prophet Haggai is contemporary with the prophet Zachariah. Their ministries were to the remnant that had returned from Babylon following the decree by Cyrus, King of Persia. The book of Haggai spans a short four month period (Hag. 1:1, 2:1, 2:10).

Historical Setting: Haggai returned to the Promised Land from Babylonian captivity under the first wave of Jews, numbering about 50,000, under the leadership of Zerubbabel (Ezra 2:1, 2).

Two years later, the foundation of the temple was laid amid praises and tears (Ezra 3:8-13), and the prospect of the temple building looked bright. However, there arose a group of people that remained in the land known as the Samaritans, who thought to stop the work on the temple of the LORD by misrepresenting the intentions of the Jews (Ezra 4:1, 5-7). Through their deceit, they were successful in stopping the work of the LORD for some 14 years (Ezra 4:24).

It was at the end of this time that God called the prophets Haggai and Zachariah to stir up the people of God from their complacency and apathy with the words, *"Consider your ways"* (Hag. 1:5, 7, 2:15, 18), and within four short years the temple was built (Ezra 4:24; 5:1 cf. Ezra 6:14, 15). Thus, both Haggai and Zachariah started their ministries in the second year of Darius (Haggai 1:1 cf. Zech. 1:1).

CHAPTER ONE

In the second year of Darius the king, in the sixth month, in the first day of the month, came the word of the LORD by Haggai the prophet unto Zerubbabel the son of Shealtiel, governor of Judah, and to Joshua the son of Josedech, the high priest, saying, Thus speaketh the LORD of hosts, saying, This people say, The time is not come, the time that the LORD'S house should be built. Then came the word of the LORD by Haggai the prophet, saying, Is it time for you, O ye, to dwell in your cieled houses, and this house lie waste? Now therefore thus saith the LORD of hosts; Consider your ways. Ye have sown much, and bring in little; ye eat, but ye have not enough; ye drink, but ye are not filled with drink; ye clothe you, but there is none warm; and he that earneth wages earneth wages to put it into a bag with holes. Thus saith the LORD of hosts; Consider your ways. Go up to the mountain, and bring wood, and build the house; and I will take pleasure in it, and I will be glorified, saith the LORD. Ye looked for much, and, lo, it came to little; and when ye brought it home, I did blow upon it. Why? saith the LORD of hosts. Because of mine house that is waste, and ye run every man unto his own house. Therefore the heaven over you is stayed from dew, and the earth is stayed from her fruit. And I called for a drought upon the land, and upon the mountains, and upon the corn, and upon the new wine, and upon the oil, and upon that which the ground bringeth forth, and upon men, and upon cattle, and upon all the labour of the hands. (Haggai 1:1-11)

What the People Say (1-5): The remnant of Jews had grown complacent due to the constant resistance from their adversaries in the land, to the point that they had convinced themselves that the LORD must not want the temple of the LORD built. They said, "The time is not come, the time that the LORD'S house should be built" (2). We need to be careful not to interpret opposition as a sign that the LORD wants us not to proceed in a direction. These Jewish people misinterpreted, assuming the LORD must have been telling them not to build His house. They were wrong, and the LORD raised up both Zachariah and Haggai to make that truth known.

The LORD answers back the apathetic Jewish remnant with, "Is it a time for you, O ye to dwell in your ceiled houses, and this house lie waste" (4).

The rebuke was that the Jewish remnant had built their own houses, but the house of the LORD had remained in a state of ruin and disrepair. Thus the LORD is telling them to "consider their ways" (5).

While they may have had shelter for their families, the LORD had withheld the weather and wealth for their disobedience (6-11).

Then Zerubbabel the son of Shealtiel, and Joshua the son of Josedech, the high priest, with all the remnant of the people, obeyed the voice of the LORD their God, and the words of Haggai the prophet, as the LORD their God had sent him, and the people did fear before the LORD. Then spake Haggai the LORD'S messenger in the LORD'S message unto the people, saying, I am with you, saith the LORD. And the LORD stirred up the spirit of Zerubbabel the son of Shealtiel, governor of Judah, and the spirit of Joshua the son of Josedech, the high priest, and the spirit of all the remnant of the people; and they came and did work in the house of the LORD of hosts, their God, In the four and twentieth day of the sixth month, in the second year of Darius the king. (Haggai 1:12-15)

Adherence to the Prophets of God (12-15): Twenty-three days of preaching leads to the people obeying the voice of the LORD, and they resume the work on the house of the LORD (12-15). Once the people obeyed the voice of the LORD, He tells them that they will not be doing the work by themselves but, "I am with you, saith the LORD" (13).

CHAPTER TWO

In the seventh month, in the one and twentieth day of the month, came the word of the LORD by the prophet Haggai, saying, Speak now to Zerubbabel the son of Shealtiel, governor of Judah, and to Joshua the son of Josedech, the high priest, and to the residue of the people, saying, Who is left among you that saw this house in her first glory? and how do ye see it now? is it not in your eyes in comparison of it as nothing? Yet now be strong, O Zerubbabel, saith the LORD; and be strong, O Joshua, son of Josedech, the high priest; and be strong, all ye people of the land, saith the LORD, and work: for I am with you, saith the LORD of hosts: According to the word that I covenanted with you when ye came out of Egypt, so my spirit remaineth among you: fear ye not. For thus saith the LORD of hosts; Yet once, it is a little while, and I will shake the heavens, and the earth, and the sea, and the dry land; And I will shake all nations, and the desire of all nations shall come: and I will fill this house with glory, saith the LORD of hosts. The silver is mine, and the gold is mine, saith the LORD of hosts. The glory of this latter house shall be greater than of the former, saith the LORD of hosts: and in this place will I give peace, saith the LORD of hosts. (Haggai 2:1-9)

Two Houses Compared (1-9): About one month later the LORD tells the people to take note of the temple they are building, asking them to compare it to the glory of the first house (Solomon's Temple) (1-3); "is it not in your eyes as nothing, says the LORD." The LORD is letting them know that though He will be with them in building this temple, it will not see the glory that God intends it to have. There is a future house of the LORD that will be built that will be filled with great glory by the LORD (7). This future house of the LORD and its glory will be at the time following when the LORD shall come and "shake the heavens and the earth and the sea and the dry land" (6). It will be a time when the LORD will cause all nations to bring their wealth or glory unto the house of the LORD (7-8 cf. Isaiah 60). It will be this latter house of the LORD that will see the greater glory of the LORD, compared to the one they are building at the time of Haggai's ministry (9).

In the four and twentieth day of the ninth month, in the second year of Darius, came the word of the LORD by Haggai the prophet, saying, Thus saith the LORD of hosts; Ask now the priests concerning the law, saying, If one bear holy flesh in the skirt of his garment, and with his skirt do touch bread, or pottage, or wine, or oil, or any meat, shall it be holy? And the priests answered and said, No. Then said Haggai, If one that is unclean by a dead body touch any of these, shall it be unclean? And the priests answered and said, It shall be unclean. Then answered Haggai, and said, So is this people, and so is this nation before me, saith the LORD; and so is every work of their hands; and that which they offer there is unclean. And now, I pray you, consider from this day and upward, from before a stone was laid upon a stone in the temple of the LORD: Since those days were, when one came to an heap of twenty measures, there were but ten: when one came to the pressfat for to draw out fifty vessels out of the press, there were but twenty. I smote you with blasting and with mildew and with hail in all the labours of your hands; yet ye turned not to me, saith the LORD. Consider now from this day and upward, from the four and twentieth day of the ninth month, even from the day that the foundation of the LORD'S temple was laid, consider it. Is the seed yet in the barn? yea, as yet the vine, and the fig tree, and the pomegranate, and the olive tree, hath not brought forth: from this day will I bless you. (Haggai 2:10-19)

The Unrighteous Works of the People (10-19): The LORD now cautions the people through the Priests, using the law of defilement as an example (12). The first example is that of a Priest carrying "holy flesh," that is flesh offered to God (animal sacrifice). If the skirt of the Priest carrying that "holy flesh" come into contact with other things of the tabernacle, does that contact make those items holy? The answer is no (12 cf. Lev. 6:27). The second example is if a Priest defile himself with a dead body and touch other items will not that make those items unclean? The answer is yes (13 cf. Lev. 19:22). Haggai now takes this and applies it to the people saying, "…so is every work of their hands; and that which they offer there is unclean" (14). Upon the return of the Jewish people they performed sacrifices to the LORD even though they had no temple (Ezra 3:3-6). Yet, all their outward practices and religious duties did not make the people clean from their willful disobedience in not building the temple of the LORD and following the laws of God in their lives (14). Thus, the LORD is calling upon them to "consider from this day and upward" what He has allowed to happen to them and their livelihood, in not blessing their crops (16-19).

And again the word of the LORD came unto Haggai in the four and twentieth day of the month, saying, Speak to Zerubbabel, governor of Judah, saying, I will shake the heavens and the earth; And I will overthrow the throne of kingdoms, and I will destroy the strength of the kingdoms of the heathen; and I will overthrow the chariots, and those that ride in them; and the horses and their riders shall come down, every one by the sword of his brother. In that day, saith the LORD of hosts, will I take thee, O Zerubbabel, my servant, the son of Shealtiel, saith the LORD, and will make thee as a signet: for I have chosen thee, saith the LORD of hosts. (Haggai 2:20-23)

Encouraging Words for Zerubbabel (20-23): This passage tells us the house of the LORD will be built by the encouragement of Zerubbabel and others. However, Zerubbabel and those others will not see the glory of the LORD fill the temple. The temple will not see the glory of the Gentile nations brought to it. The house of the LORD will see a great and glorious future one day, and the LORD graciously tells Zerubbabel that he will be a part of that glorious time (23).

CONCLUSION

Haggai's ministry though lasting only four short months is vital in motivation the people of God to get busy completing the house of God. For some fourteen plus years they work had ceased due mostly to adversaries in the land. However, in the second year of Darius the LORD raises up Haggai and Zachariah to exhort and rebuke the people. Haggai calls upon the people to "consider their ways" concerning the work of the LORD and by the grace of God the people listen to the voice of God and in four short years complete the work that laid dormant for so long.

Bibliography

Keller, Werner. The Bible As History. New York: Bantam, 1982.

Josephus, Flavius. The Works of Flavius Josephus, Volume III. Grand Rapids: Baker Book House, 1974

Kennedy, Kurt. The Book of Ezekiel, The Glory of the Lord has Departed. Seattle: True Word Press, 2015.

The Prophets of the Post Exile: Haggai, Zechariah & Malachi. CD-ROM, 20081997. Dr. Chuck Missler

"Zechariah, Israel Behold Your King." *Truthnet.org*. 2012

Kennedy, Kurt. The Book of Daniel Study Helps. Seattle: True Word Press, 2015.